Contents

Front Cover: Woking Village

Introduction

This bibliography is intended primarily for genealogists. It is, however, hoped that it will also prove useful to historians, librarians, archivists, research students, and anyone else interested in the history of Surrey and Sussex. It is intended to be used in conjunction with my *English genealogy: a bibliography,* with the other volumes of *Surrey and Sussex: the genealogists' library guide,* and with the companion volumes in the *British genealogical library guides* series. A full list of these volumes currently in print appears on the back cover.

Published sources of information on Surrey and Sussex genealogy are listed in volumes 1-5 of the present work; this volume lists works devoted to the history of specific families, together with collections of pedigrees, biographical dictionaries, diaries & letters, and heraldry. It includes published books and journal articles, but excludes the innumerable notes and queries to be found in the many family history society journals, except where their content is of importance. Where I have included such notes, replies to them are cited in the form 'see also', with no reference to the names of respondents. I have also excluded extracts from newspapers, and works which have not been published. Where possible, citations are accompanied by notes indicating the period covered, the locality/ies in which the families concerned dwelt, and other pertinent information. I have physically examined almost every item listed here; those which have not been seen are annotated 'not seen', as I have not been able to check the correct title or the contents. Pedigrees and family histories contained in works on other genealogical topics, and listed in other volumes of this library guide, are, in general, excluded here; all six volumes are intended to be used together.

Be warned: just because information has been published, it does not necessarily follow that it is accurate. I have not made any judgement on the accuracy of most works listed: that is up to you.

Anyone who tries to compile a totally comprehensive bibliography of Surrey and Sussex is likely to fall short of his aim. The task is almost impossible, especially if the endeavour is made by one person. That does not, however, mean that the attempt should not be made. This book is as

4

comprehensive as I have been able to make it. However, usefulness, rather than comprehensiveness, has been my prime aim – and this book would not be useful to anyone if its publication were to be prevented by a vain attempt to ensure total comprehensiveness. I am well aware that there are likely to be omissions, especially in view of the fact that, given constraints of time and money, it has not been possible for me to visit all of the large number of libraries with substantial collections on the history of Surrey and Sussex. Each of them may well possess works not held anywhere else. The identification of such works is not, however, a major aim of this bibliography. Rather, my purpose has been to enable you to identify works which are mostly readily available. Some titles you may be able to purchase; all can be found in libraries throughout the English-speaking world. You can check the holdings of many libraries via their catalogues on the internet; alternatively, if your local library does not hold a particular book, the librarian should be able to tell you where to find it – and, as a last resort, may be able to borrow if for you via the inter-library loan network, irrespective of whether you live in London or San Francisco. The libraries of family history societies are also worth checking – even if they are far distant from Surrey and Sussex: for example, the Genealogical Society of Victoria, in Melbourne, has a good collection of books on English genealogy. Some family history societies offer a postal borrowing service; others may be willing to check a particular book for you. It is also worth joining one of the genealogical newsgroups or mailing lists on the internet; other members may hold the books you need, and be willing to check them for you.

If you are an assiduous researcher, you may well come across items I have missed. If you do, please let me know, so that they can be included in the next edition.

The work of compiling this bibliography has depended heavily on the resources of the libraries I have used. These included the Surrey History Centre, and local studies collections in the public libraries of Worthing, Chichester, Brighton, Eastbourne, Hastings, Richmond, Brixton, Croydon, and Southwark, as well as West Sussex Record Office. I have also relied heavily on the Society of Genealogists, the University of Exeter, Exeter Public Library, the British Library, and the Society of Genealogists, All these institutions deserve my thanks, as do Cliff Webb & Martin Hayes, who both read and commented on an early draft of the book. Cynthia Hanson typed the manuscript, and Bob Boyd saw the book through the press. I am grateful too to the officers of the Federation of Family History Societies, whose support is vital for the continuation of this series. My thanks also to my wife Marjorie.

Stuart A. Raymond

Abbreviations

B.R.L.H.S.N.	*Bognor Regis Local History Society newsletter*
D.P.H.S.M.	*Danehill Parish Historical Society magazine*
E.L.H.	*Eastbourne Local Historian*
E.L.H.S.N.	*Eastbourne Local History Society newsletter*
E.Sy.F.H.S.J.	*East Surrey Family History Society journal*
F.M.S.Q.N.	*Farnham Museum Society quarterly newsletter*
F.H.S.	Family History Society
F.R.	*Family Roots*
H. & R.F.H.S.J.	*Hastings & Rother Family History Society [journal]*
L.H.R.	*Local history records for Caterham and Warlingham, Coulsdon and Purley [Bourne Society local history records]*
M.G.H.	*Miscellanea genealogica et heraldica*
N.S.	New Series
P.L.D.L.H.S.	*Proceedings of the Leatherhead & District Local History Society*
P.R.S.	Parish Register Society
R. & B.	*Root and branch [West Surrey F.H.S. journal]*
R.H.	*Richmond history*
Sx.A.C	*Sussex archaeological collections*
Sx.A.S.N.	*Sussex Archaeological Society newsletter*
Sx.F.H.	*Sussex family historian*
Sx.G.L.H.	*Sussex genealogist and local historian*
Sx.N.Q.	*Sussex notes and queries*
Sx.R.S.	Sussex Record Society
Sy.A.C	*Surrey archaeological collections*
Sy.R.S.	Surrey Record Society
W.Sx.H.	*West Sussex history*

Bibliographic Presentation

Authors' names are in SMALL CAPITALS. Book and journal titles are in *italics*. Articles appearing in journals, and essays, *etc.,* forming only parts of books, are in inverted commas. Volume numbers are shown in **bold,** and the individual numbers of journals may be shown in parentheses. In the case of articles, further figures indicate page numbers. Book titles are normally followed by the place of publication (except where this is London, which is omitted), the name of the publisher, and the date of publication.

Libraries and Record Offices

There are numerous libraries with substantial book collections relating to Surrey and Sussex. For the present (post-1974) county of Surrey, the major library is the Surrey History Centre; however, boundary changes mean that there are also 6 London metropolitan boroughs in historic Surrey, all of which have specialist local history collections. Most public libraries also have some local history materials.

For Sussex, most of the major town libraries have substantial local history collections, as do the Record Offices of East and West Sussex. The libraries at Worthing and Brighton probably have the most substantial collections.

Collections relating to Surrey and Sussex may also be found in many other public and university libraries throughout the country (and, indeed, the world), as well as at specialist institutions such as the Society of Genealogists and the British Library. The local family history societies also have small libraries.

The list which follows concentrates on those libraries within the historic counties, and is very selective.

SURREY

Surrey History Centre,
130, Goldsworth Road,
Woking,
Surrey, GU21 1ND

Croydon
Croydon Library & Archives Service,
Katharine Street,
Croydon,
Surrey, CR9 1ET

Kingston on Thames
Local History Centre,
Heritage Centre,
Wheatfield Way,
Kingston on Thames,
Surrey, KT1 2PS

Lambeth
Minet Library,
52, Knatchbull Road,
Brixton,
London, SE5 9QY

Merton
Merton Local Studies Centre,
Merton Civic Centre,
London Road,
Morden,
Surrey, SM4 5DX

Richmond
Richmond Local Studies Library,
Central Reference Library,
Old Town Hall,
Whittaker Avenue,
Richmond,
Surrey, TW9 1TP

Southwark
Southwark Local Studies Library,
211, Borough High Street,
Southwark,
London,
SE1 1JA

Sutton
Sutton Archives,
Central Library,
St.Nicholas Way,
Sutton,
Surrey,
SM1 1EA

Wandsworth
Wandsworth Local History Collection,
Battersea Library,
265, Lavender Hill
London, SW11 1JB

SUSSEX
East Sussex Record Office,
The Maltings,
Castle Precincts,
Lewes,
Sussex, BN7 1YT

West Sussex Record Office,
County Hall,
Chichester,
PO19 1RN

Brighton
Brighton Local Studies Library,
Church Street,
Brighton,
Sussex, BN1 1UD

Chichester
Local Studies Collection,
West Sussex County Library,
Tower Street,
Chichester,
Sussex, PO19 1QJ

Eastbourne
Local Studies Collection,
Eastbourne Library,
Grove Road,
Eastbourne,
Sussex, BN21 4LT

Hastings
Local Studies Collection,
Hastings Library,
Brassey Institute,
13, Claremont,
Hastings, TN34 1HE

Lewes
Sussex Room,
Lewes Library,
Albion Street,
Lewes,
Sussex, BN7 2ND

Worthing
Local Studies Library,
Worthing Library,
Richmond Road,
Worthing,
Sussex, BN11 1HD

1. PEDIGREE COLLECTIONS (INCLUDING HERALDIC VISITATIONS)

The modern genealogist is fortunate in being able to draw on the work of his predecessors. Many nineteenth century antiquaries made collections of pedigrees, some of which were published. A number of the latter are national in scope and are listed in Raymond's *English genealogy: a bibliography*, section 7. For Surrey and Sussex, the works of Berry and Comber are particularly useful. Of course, most of the pedigrees given in these tomes relate to the gentry — but don't let that put you off. Many gentry rose from humble beginnings, and many others married beneath them, or were otherwise 'reduced in circumstances.'

BERRY, WILLIAM. *County genealogies: pedigrees of Surrey families*. Sherwood, Gilbert and Piper, 1837.

BERRY, WILLIAM. *Pedigrees of the families in the County of Sussex collected from the heraldic visitations and other authentic manuscripts in the British Museum, and in the possession of private individuals, and from the information of the present resident families*. Sherwood Gilbert & Piper, 1830.

COMBER, JOHN. *Sussex genealogies: Ardingly Centre*. Cambridge: W. Heffer & Sons, 1932.

COMBER, JOHN. *Sussex genealogies: Horsham Centre*. Cambridge: W. Heffer & Sons, 1931.

COMBER, JOHN. *Sussex genealogies: Lewes Centre*. Cambridge: W. Heffer & Sons, 1933.

See also:

ELLIS, WILLIAM SMITH. 'On the origin of some Sussex families', *Sx.A.C.* 24, 1872, 25-40. Brief notes on 20 families.

HART, WILLIAM HENRY, & HOWARD, JOSEPH JACKSON. 'Genealogical and heraldic memoranda relating to the County of Surrey, vol.II', *Sy.A.C.* 2, 1864, unpaginated. Includes pedigrees of Clifton of Worplesdon; Parkhurst of Guildford; Abbot of Guildford; Cole of Petersham; Knightly of Kingston; Banester of Croydon; Tonstall of Addiscombe; Waterer of Woking; Bradbridge of Lambeth; Burton of Carshalton.

LOWER, MARK ANTONY. 'Notes on old Sussex families', *Sx.A.C.* 24, 1872, 1-24; 25, 1873, 101-11.

In the sixteenth and seventeenth centuries, the heralds undertook 'visitations' of the counties in order to determine the right of gentry to bear arms. This necessitated the compilation of pedigrees, which continue to be major sources of genealogical information. A number of pedigree collections and associated documents from these heraldic visitations relating to Surrey and Sussex have been published.

Surrey

BANNERMAN, W. BRUCE, ed. *The visitations of the County of Surrey made and taken in the years 1530 by Thomas Benolte, Clarenceux King of arms, 1572 by Robert Cooke, Clarenceux King of arms, and 1623 by Samuel Thompson, Windsor Herald, and Augustin Vincent Rouge Croix pursuivant, marshals and deputies to William Camden, Clarenceux King of arms*. Publications of the Harleian Society 43. 1899.

Sussex

CRAWFORD, G.P. 'Heraldic visitations of Sussex', *Sussex county magazine* 47, 1930, 202-5. General discussion.

HOWARD, JOSEPH JACKSON, ed. *The visitacon of Surry made A° 1623 by Samuell Thompson, Windsor Herauld, and Augustyne of Vincent, Rougcroix, marshalls and deputies to Wm. Camden esq., Clarenceux King of Armes*. Published as supplement to, and sometimes bound with, *Sy.A.C.* 2-12. 1865-93.

ARMYTAGE, GEORGE J., ed. *A visitation of the County of Surrey, begin anno dni MDCLXII, finished anno dni MDCLXVIII*. Publications of the Harleian Society 60. 1910.

'Addenda to the printed visitation of Sussex from Harleian ms. 1076 in the British Museum', *M.G.H.* 5th series 2-3, 1916-19, *passim*.

BAX, A. RIDLEY. 'Disclaimers at the Heralds' visitations in the reign of James I', *Sy.A.C.* 18, 1903, 217-9. List.

11

BANNERMAN, W. BRUCE, ed. *The visitations of the County of Sussex made and taken in the years 1530, by Thomas Benolte, Clarenceux King of Arms, and 1633-4, by John Philipot, Somerset Herald, and George Owen, York Herald, for Sir John Burroughs, Garter, and Sir Richard St. George, Clarenceux.* Publications of the Harleian Society **53**. 1905.

CLARKE, A.W.HUGHES, ed. *The visitation of Sussex anno domini 1662, made by Sir Edward Bysshe, Clarenceux King of arms.* Publications of the Harleian Society **89**. 1937.

CLARKE, A.W.HUGHES. *Addenda to the printed Visitations of Sussex from Harleian ms. 1076 in the British Museum.* Mitchell Hughes and Clarke, 1929. Reprinted from *M.G.H.,* with additional indexes.

PECKHAM, W.D. 'The first and last heraldic visitations of Sussex', *Sx.N.Q.* **2**, 1929, 202-7. Index to the (unpublished) visitation of 1662-8.

For a description of a current index to pedigrees, which every Sussex genealogist should consult, see:

HILDER, IAN. 'An introduction to the Sussex pedigrees index: has my family been researched before? *Sx.F.H.* **12**(3), 1996, 109-11. Covering research in progress, published pedigrees, and manuscript pedigree collections.

2. BIOGRAPHICAL DICTIONARIES

Who's who must be one of the most frequently consulted book on our library shelves today. It may stand as representative of the thousands of biographical dictionaries that are available, and that are likely to provide useful information for genealogists. A variety of lists and indexes, *etc.,* of these dictionaries are identified in Raymond's *English genealogy: a bibliography,* and should be consulted. A number of biographical dictionaries relating specifically to Surrey and Sussex are available. Some of these are contemporary, i.e. they include the lives of people living at the time they were compiled; others are retrospective, covering the whole span of history. There are also a few works offering brief lives of people in specific places within the two counties.

Who's who in Kent, Surrey and Sussex, 1911. Horace Cox, 1911.

Surrey
The County of Surrey, with illustrated biographies. St. Albans: Truman Press, 1896. Biograpical dictionary of contemporay leading figures.

PRESS, C.A.MANNING. *Surrey leaders, social and political.* De Vere & Co., 1900-1901.

GASKELL, ERNEST. *Surrey leaders, social and political.* Queenhithe Printing and Publishing Co., [190-?]

GRANT, JOHN. *Surrey, historical biographical and pictorial.* London & Provincial Publishing Co., [190-].

HITCHIN, W.E. *Surrey at the opening of the twentieth century.* Pike's new century series **18**. Brighton: W.T.Pike & Co., 1906. Includes W.T. Pike, ed. *Contemporary biographies,* which is reprinted in facsimile in:

HITCHIN, W.E. & PIKE, W.T. *A dictionary of Edwardian biography: Surrey.* Edinburgh. Peter Bell, 1987.

Who's who in Surrey. Worcester: Ebenezer Baylis & Son, 1936.

HIME, JANET. *People of Surrey.* Debretts Peerage, 1991. Not seen.

Ashtead

LEVER, R.A. 'Notes on some Ashtead personalites, 1543-1732', *P.L.D.L.H.S.* 4(10), 1986, 284-9. Biographical notes in dictionary format.

Barnes & Mortlake

GILL, RAYMOND CLARIDGE. *A dictionary of local celebrities.* 2nd ed. Barnes & Mortlake Historical Society, 1980.

Clapham

SMITH, ERIC E.F. *Clapham saints and sinners: extracts from the occasional sheets of the Clapham Antiquarian Society.* Clapham Press, 1987. Many brief biographies, including a pedigree of Thornton.

Guildford, *etc.*

Who's who in Guildford, Godalming and Woking. Pullman Press, 1960.

Peckham

BEASLEY, JOHN D. *Who was who in Peckham: personalities of the past and present who had links with Peckham in South London.* Chener Books, 1985.

MOULD, RICHARD W. *Southwark men of mark, past and present: a contribution towards a dictionary of Southwark biography,* ed. Robert Woodger Bowers. Bowers Brothers, 1905. Biographical dictionary.

Wandsworth

'Obituary notices of Wandsworth worthies, *Gentlemans magazine* 1731-1780', *Wandsworth notes and queries* 7, 1899, 134-7. List.

Sussex

LOWER, MARK ANTONY. *The worthies of Sussex: biographical sketches of the most eminent natives or inhabitants of the county, from the earliest period to the present time.* Lewes: Geo. P. Bacon, 1865.

The County of Sussex and many of its family records. Exeter: Wiliam Pollard & Co., 1898. Contempoprary biographies of eminent persons.

SEARLE, SHARON. *Sussex women, famous, infamous, unsung.* Tunbridge Wells: J.A.K.Books, 1995. 35 brief biographies.

Sussex: historical, biographical, pictorial. [ ]: Allan North, 1907.

PIKE, W.T. *A dictionary of contemporary biography: Sussex.* Edinburgh: Peter Bell, 1987. Facsimile reprint of the biographical portion of *Sussex in the twentieth century: contemporary biographies,* originally published Brighton: W.T. Pike, 1910.

Who's who in Sussex. Worcester: Ebenezer Baylis & Sons, 1935.

HIME, JULIET, ed. *People of Sussex.* Debretts Peerage, 1991. Contemporary biographical dictionary.

Hastings

PLAINE, G. *Notables and innkeepers, etc., of Hastings.* Hastings & Rother F.H.S., 1989. Lists of M.P's, borough officers, shipwrights, ropemakers, sailmakers, seamen, fishermen, many innkeepers, *etc.*

Tuxlith

CHATTERTON-NEWMAN, ROGER. *Tuxlith worthies: men and women who have influenced the history of Rake and Milland and of their nation.* Tuxlith tracts 4. Milland: Friends of Tuxlith Chapel, 1996. Brief biographies of rectors and curates of Trotton cum Tuxlith, vicars of Milland, manorial lords, patrons of the living, and chapelwardens.

Westbourne

HOGG, DAVID. *Westbourne worthies.* Bygone Westbourne 8. Westbourne: Westbourne Local History Group. 1996. Brief biographies.

Worthing

WIGHTWICK, DUDLEY, ed. *Who's who in Worthing and district 1938-1940.* Ludovic Grant & Co., [1938?]

3. HERALDRY.

A. General

The study of heraldry may be useful to the genealogist, if ancestor(s) were entitled to bear arms. For a substantial introduction to the subject for Sussex, (nothing similar is available for Surrey) see:

HUXFORD, J.F. *Arms of Sussex families.* Phillimore, 1982.

See also:

ATTREE, F.W.T. 'Lists of Sussex gentry at various dates with descriptions of the arms of a few families not previously noticed', *Sx.A.C.* **39**, 1894, 99-133.

ANDRÉ, J. LEWIS. 'Heraldry and Sussex monuments', *Sx.A.C.* **37**, 1890, 1-16. See also **38**, 1892, 197-8. General discussion.

ELLIS, WILLIAM SMITH. 'Budgen's unofficial heraldic visitation of Sussex, 1724, with an introduction and notes', *Sx.A.C.* **25**, 1873, 85-100. Gives arms of 150 families.

ELLIS, WILLIAM SMITH. 'Early Sussex armory', *Sx.A.C.* **30**, 1880, 137-46.

ELLIS, W.S. 'On the origin of the arms of some Sussex families', *Sx.A.C.* **6**, 1853, 71-89.

ELLIS, W. SMITH. 'On the origin of the arms of some Sussex families, second series, *Sx.A.C.* **37**, 1890, 17-38.

HALL, HELENA. 'Arms of some famous Sussex families', *Sussex county magazine* **10**, 1936, 622-6, 686-9, 762-5 & 802-5. Identifies 40 arms.

HALL, HELENA. 'Punning in some Sussex coats of arms', *Sussex county magazine* **15**, 1941, 56-9.

B. Grants of arms and family heraldry etc.

Blackman

FLETCHER, W.G.D. 'Docquets of grants of arms', *Genealogist* N.S., **22**, 1906, 154-8. Includes grant to George Blackman of Surrey, 1803.

Blount

HUMPHERY-SMITH, C.R. 'The Blount quarters', *Coat of arms* **4**(30), 1957, 224-7. Medieval; includes pedigree.

Bolney

'Grant of crest by Thomas Holney, Clarenceux, to John Bolney of Bolney, Co.Sussex, esquire, 1541', *M.G.H.* **1**, 1868, 304.

Bruere

'Grant of arms by Sir Isaac Heard, Kt., Garter, and George Harrison, Clarenceux, to William Bruere of Ashted, 1803', *M.G.H.* **2**, 1876, 20-21.

Bysshe

ELLIOT, H.L. 'The armorials in glass at the Colchester Museum', *Transactions of the Essex Archaeological Society* N.S., **11**, 1911, 21-6. Bysshe family of Burstow, Surrey; includes folded pedigree, 14-17th c.

Cooke

'Grant of arms: Ralph Cooke, D.D., 1662', *M.G.H.* 5th series **8**, 1932-4, 135.

Covert

See Goring

Dee

'Grants and confirmation of arms and crest', *M.G.H.* 5th series **8**, 1932-4, 261-4. Includes grant to John Dee of Mortlake, 1576.

Devenish

LAMBARDE, FANE. 'The heraldry of Horselunges', *Sx.A.C.* **69**, 1928, 71-6. Arms of the Devenish family, *etc.*

Evershed

'Confirmation of arms by Sir Thomas St. George, Garter, and Sir Henry St. George, Clarenceaux, to John Evershed of Evershed 1696', *M.G.H.* **2**, 1876, 191-2.

Garthwaite

'Confirmation of arms to Edward Garthwaite of Shakleford, 1748', *M.G.H.* N.S., **4**, 1884, 422.

Gavell

'Coat of arms to Robert Gavell of Cobham, in the County of Surrey, 12th August 1572', *Sy.A.C.* **3**, 1865, 349-50.

'Grant of arms to Robert Gauell of Cobham, in the County of Surrey, 12th August 1572', *M.G.H.* N.S. **1**, 1874, 320-1.

Goring
LAMBARDE, FANE. 'Notes on the heraldry of Goring and Covert', *Sx.A.C.* **68**,, 1927, 79-88. See also **69**, 1928, 230.

Greene
'Grant of arms to William Greene, esq., of Mitcham, Surrey, 6th January 1663', *Sy.A.C.* **3**, 1865, 350-51.

Grose
'Grant of arms to Francis Grose, Richmond Herald, 1756', *M.G.H.* N.S., **4**, 1885, 1-2. Of Richmond.

Hubbard
'Grant of arms to William Hubbard, esq., 1707', *M.G.H.* 2nd series **4**, 1892, 177.

Kenrick
'Kenrick bookplates', *M.G.H.* 5th series **9**, 1935-7, 102. Of London and Surrey, 17-19th c.

Lawrence
'Grant of arms to Sir Paul Ogden Lawrence, one of the justices of his Majesty's High Court of Justice, and the other descendants of his family', *M.G.H.* 5th series **4**, 1920-22, 178-9. Of Wandsworth, 1919.

Leechford
'Leechford of Shelwood', *M.G.H.* **1**, 1868, 34-5. 1605. Arms.

Lewknor
LAMBARDE, FANE. 'The Lewknor carpet', *Sx.A.C.* **70**, 1929, 1-7. Heraldic carpet, 16th c.
LAMBARDE, FANE. 'A Lewknor seal', *Sx.N.Q.* **2**, 1929, 151. Heraldry, 14th c.

Mawbey
'Grant of arms to Joseph Mawbey of Kennington, 1757', *M.G.H.* N.S., **3**, 1880, 447.

More
ATTREE, F.W.T. 'Arms of More of Morehouse', *Sx.A.C.* **36**, 1888, 248-9. Medieval.

Northland
'Grant of arms to Thomas Northland of the County of Sussex, gentleman, dated London, 10 November, 22 Edward IV', *M.G.H.* 2nd series **4**, 1892, 144(f). Facsimile.

Paltock
'Confirmation of arms, and grant of crest, to Edward Paltock of Kingston-on-Thames, 14th February, 9 James I', *Sy.A.C.* **3**, 1865, 351-2.

Parker
KING, THOMAS WILLIAM. 'Notices of grants of an augmentation to the arms of Archbishop Parker, and of a crest to his son John Parker', *Sy.A.C.* **2**, 1864, 203-9. Includes pedigree of Parker, 15-16th c.; originally of Norwich.

Parvis
'Confirmation of arms to Henry Parvis, of the County of Surrey, 3rd December 1597', *Sy.A.C.* **3**, 1865, 352.

Payne
CRAWFORD, G.P. 'Grant of arms and crest to Edward Payne and his brothers of East Grinstead, 1661', *M.G.H.* 5th series **6**, 1926-8, 49.

Pelham
LOWER, MARK ANTONY. 'Observations on the buckle: the badge of the family of Pelham, and its application to various ecclesiastical buildings in Sussex, and on the badge of the family of De La Warr', *Sx.A.C.* **3**, 1850, 211-31. Medieval - 17th c.
SALZMAN, L.F. 'The early heraldry of Pelham', *Sx.A.C.* **69**, 1928, 53-70. Includes pedigrees, 14-15th c.

Pilfold
'Grant of arms to Captain John Pilfold, R.N., 1808', *M.G.H.* N.S., **4**, 1884, 75-7. Of Horsham.

Poole
'Confirmation of the arms of Poole',
Genealogist **5,** 1881, 116. Of Sussex, 1648.

Puckle
'Grants and confirmations of arms and
crests', *M.G.H.* 5th series **10,** 1938, 101-3.
Includes grant to Puckle of Sussex.

Sheldon
'Grant of arms by Sir William Dugdale,
Garter' to Daniel Sheldon of Ham Court,
1681', *M.G.H.* N.S., **1,** 1874, 371-2.

Skuse
SKUSE, PETER R. 'A coat of arms', *L.H.R.*
33, 1994, 25-9. Granted to the author.

Sullivan
JEWERS, ARTHUR J. 'Sullivan bookplates',
M.G.H. 5th series **2,** 1917, 297-8.
Discussion of incorrect arms on
bookplates.

Upton
'Grant of crest to William Upton, 1569',
M.G.H. 2nd series **5,** 1894, 296. Of Sussex
and Devon.

Weston
WESTON, HENRY M. 'Arms of the Westons in
West Clandon church', *Sy.A.C.* **22,** 1909,
196-7.

Whitgift
OUSELEY, M.H. 'Notes on the right arms of
John Whitgift, Lord Archbishop of
Canterbury, 1583-1604', *Sy.A.C.* **63,** 1966,
95-129.

C. Funeral Certificates

Evelyn
'Genealogical memoranda relating to the
family of Evelyn', *M.G.H.* 2nd series **1,**
1886, 1-2. Includes funeral certificate of
John Evelyn of Godstone, 1627.

Gresham
'Funeral certificates', *M.G.H.* **2,** 1876, 317-20.
Includes certificate of Sir Thomas
Gresham of Titsey, 1630.

Hall
RYLANDS, J. PAUL. 'Funeral certificate of
Thomas Hall of Godalming, Surrey',
M.G.H. 4th series **1,** 1906, 194. 1623.

Heron
'Funeral certificate of Sir Nicholas Heron,
1568', *Sy.A.C.* **10,** 1891, 141-2.

Lee
'Funeral certificate: Mrs. Elizabeth Lee,
1624', *M.G.H.* 2nd series **5,** 1894, 304.

4. DIARIES, LETTERS, HOUSEHOLD ACCOUNTS, etc.

Diaries, letters, and household accounts all record contemporary events, and frequently contain information of genealogical value, e.g. mention of births, marriages and deaths. They deserve to be consulted by all genealogists, and not just those researching the particular families which produced them. For a full listing of Sussex diaries, see:
BURCHALL, MICHAEL J. *A catalogue of Sussex diaries.* Occasional papers **9**. Brighton: Sussex Genealogical Centre, 1984.
See also:
HARWOOD, BRIAN. 'Our Sussex diarists', *Sx.G.L.H.* **5**(1), 1983, 32-8. See also **5**(2), 1983, 79; **5**(3), 1983, 121-2. List of manuscript and published diaries.
READMAN, ALAN, & MCCANN, TIMOTHY. 'Diaries in the West Sussex Record Office', *Sx.G.L.H.* **5**(4), 1984, 145-7.

Apsley
BLAAUW, W.H. 'Apsley manuscripts of the seventeenth century in the possession of Mrs. Mabbott', *Sx.A.C.* **4**, 1851, 219-30. Family letters; includes pedigree, 16-17th c.

Ashburnham
GUNNIS, RUPERT. 'Letters of the first Lord Ashburnham', *Sx.A.C.* **88**, 1949, 1-14. Brief extracts, 1695-1708.

Baker
BAKER, JOHN. *The diary of John Baker, barrister of the Middle Temple, solicitor-general of the Leeward Islands, being extracts therefrom ... a record of life, family history, and society 1751-1778 in England (mostly in Sussex and London) and the Leeward Islands, and of two travels abroad,* ed. Philip C. Yorke. Hutchinson & Co., 1931. Includes pedigree, 17-18th c.
BLUNT, WILFRID SCAWEN. 'Extracts from Mr. John Baker's Horsham diary', *Sx.A.C.* **52**, 1909, 38-82. For 1771-7.

Bates
WRIGHT, MAISIE. 'The journal of a Cuckfield clocksmith, 1793-1834', *W.Sx.H.* **25**, 1983, 31-4; **26**, 1983, 32-7. Includes brief extracts from the journal of Edward Bates.

Bax
BAX, ALFRED RIDLEY. 'Notes and extracts from the account-book of Richard Bax, a Surrey yeoman, kept between 1648-1662', *Antiquary* **6**(34), 1882, 161-6. Many names.

Buckle
READMAN, A.E. *The Buckle papers: a catalogue.* Chichester: West Sussex County Council, 1978. Correspondence, *etc.,* mainly 18-19th c. Includes folded pedigree, 16-20th c.

Burgess
SAWYER, JOHN. 'Some extracts from the journal and correspondence of Mr. John Burgess, of Ditchling, Sussex, 1785-1815', *Sx.A.C.* **40**, 1896, 131-61. See also **41**, 1898, 238-9.

Burrell
BLENCOWE, ROBERT WILLIS, ed. 'Extracts from the journal and account-book of Timothy Burrell, esq., barrister-at-law, of Ockenden House, Cuckfield, from the year 1683 to 1714', *Sx.A.C.* **3**, 1850, 117-72.

Campion
BLENCOWE, ROBERT WILLIS. 'Extracts from manuscripts in the possession of William John Campion, esq., at Danny, and Sir Thomas Maryon Wilson, Bart., of Charlton House', *Sx.A.C.* **10**, 1858, 1-52. Letters of the Campion and Wilson families, 17-18th c., includes pedigree of Campion, 16-18th c.

Carew
BAX, ALFRED RIDLEY. 'Notes and extracts from a memorandum book of Nicholas Carew (afterwards First Baronet) of Beddington, Co.Surrey, kept between 27th February 1704/5 and 5th May 1708, *Sy.A.C.* **10**, 1891, 255-72.
LAMBERT, HENRY. 'A Carew household book', *Sy.A.C.* **31**, 1918, 1-22. Accounts of Sir Francis Carew of Beddington, 1607.

Carley
CARLEY, GAINS. *The memoirs of Gains Carley, a Sussex blacksmith,* ed. Francis W.Steer. Chichester: Moore & Tillyer, 1964. Early 20th c.

Cobden
GILL, PATRICIA, ed. *The Cobden and Unwin papers: a catalogue.* Chichester: West Sussex County Record Office, 1967. Mainly correspondence, 19th c.

STEER, F.W. *The Cobden papers: a catalogue.* Chichester: West Sussex County Council, 1964. Mainly correspondence, 19th c. Includes folded pedigrees, 18-19th c.

Collier
CRAKE, W.V. 'The correspondence of John Collier five times mayor of Hastings, and his connection with the Pelham family', *Sx.A.C.* **45**, 1902, 62-109. See also **46**, 1903, 238-9. Includes pedigree shewing connexions of Collier, Milward, and Sayer, 18-19th c.

Constable
BUTTERWORTH, ERIC. 'The diary of a Ringmer vicar', *Sussex history* **1**(7), 1979, 8-13. Brief extracts from the diary of Rev. John Constable, c.1825-52.

Dawes
REDSTONE, V.B. 'The diary of Sir Thomas Dawes, 1644', *Sy.A.C.* **37**, 1926-7, 1-36. Includes notes on Dawes family births, marriages and deaths, 1571-1643.

Egerton
EGERTON, JOHN COKER. *Victorian village: the diaries of the Reverend John Coker Egerton, curate and rector of Burwash, East Sussex, 1857-1888,* ed. Roger Wells. Stroud: Alan Sutton, 1992.

Evelyn
EVELYN, JOHN. *The diary of John Evelyn,* ed. E.S. de Beer. 6 vols. Oxford. Clarendon Press, 1955. Various other editions also available. This edition includes various pedigrees of Evelyn, 15-18th c.

Everden
COOPER, WILLIAM DURRANT. 'Extracts from account-books of the Everden and Frewen families in the seventeenth century', *Sx.A.C.* **4**, 1851, 22-30.

Frewen
See Everden

Fuller
CROSSLEY, DAVID. & SAVILLE, RICHARD, eds. *The Fuller letters, 1728-1755: guns, slaves and finance.* Sx.R.S. **76**. 1991. Includes pedigree of Fuller, 16-18th c.

Gadcum
GROSSET, L. 'The account book of William Gadcum: a glimpse into the working life of a Farnham carpenter, 1754-1842', *Surrey history* **1**(4), 1976, 158-69.

Gale
BLENCOWE, R.W., ed. 'Extracts from the journal of Walter Gale, schoolmaster at Mayfield, 1750', *Sx.A.C.* **9**, 1857, 182-207.

Hawkins
STEER, FRANCIS W. *The Hawkins papers: a catalogue.* Chichester: West Sussex County Council, 1962. Mainly 18-19th c. correspondence; includes pedigree, 18-19th c.

STEER, FRANCIS W., ed. *I am, my dear Sir ... : a selection of letters written mainly to and by John Hawkins, F.R.S., F.G.S., 1761-1841, of Bignor Park, Sussex, and Trewithen, Cornwall.* [ ], 1959. Includes folded 'pedigree of the families of Hawkins, Johnstone, Waldo and Sibthorpe', 17-20th c.

Jeake
JEAKE, SAMUEL. *An astrological diary of the seventeenth century: Samuel Jeake of Rye 1652-1699,* ed. Michael Hunter & Annabel Gregory. Oxford: Clarendon Press, 1988. Includes pedigrees of Jeake, Key, Hartshorne and Hartridge.

Lee
JENKINSON, HILARY. 'A late Surrey chronicler (Surrey and the Revolution, 1688)', *Sy.A.C.* **27**, 1914, 1-20. Discussion of a notebook belonging to Lawrence Lee of Godalming, containing his autobiography, sermons, and lists of fatalities from smallpox in Godalming, 1701-30; includes pedigree of Lee, 17-19th c.

Lennard
LENNARD, T. BARRETT. 'Extracts from the household account book of Herstmonceux Castle, from August 1643 to December 1649', *Sx.A.C.* **48**, 1905, 104-37. Belonging to Francis Lennard, Lord Dacre.

Luxford
D'ELBOUX, R.H. 'The account book of George Luxford of Hellingly', *Sx.N.Q.* **12**, 1948-9, 137-41. Early 18th c.

Mantell
MANTELL, GIDEON. *The journal of Gideon Mantell, surgeon and geologist, covering the years 1818-1852* ed. E. Cecil Curwen. Oxford University Press, 1940.

Marchant
TURNER, EDWARD. 'The Marchant diary', *Sx.A.C.* **25**, 1873, 163-203. Extracts from the diary of Thomas Marchant of Hurstpierpoint, 1714-28; includes pedigree, 18-19th c.

Michell
MICHELL, HENRY. *Victorian Horsham: the diary of Henry Michell, 1809-1874,* ed. Kenneth Neale. Chichester: Phillimore & Co., 1975.

Moore
BIRD, RUTH, ed. *The journal of Giles Moore.* Sx.R.S. **68**. 1971. Rector of Horsted Keynes; journal for 1655-79.
MOORE, GILES. 'Extracts from the journal and account book of the Rev. Giles Moore, rector of Horsted Keynes, Sussex, from the year 1655 to 1679', *Sx.A.C.* **1**, 1848, 65-127.

Penn
DUNN, RICHARD S., & DUNN, MARY MAPLES, eds. *The papers of William Penn.* 5 vols. [ ]: University of Pennsylvania Press, 1981-6.

Reynolds
RICHARDSON, JOANNA, ed. *Letters from Lambeth: the correspondence of the Reynolds family with John Freeman Milward Dovaston, 1808-1815.* Royal Society of Literature, 1981.

Roe
ROE, WILLIAM. *The private memorandum of William Roe of Withdean in the County of Sussex, 1775-1809,* ed. C. Thomas-Stanford. Brighton: privately published, 1928.

Shelley
DJABRI, SUSAN CABELL, & KNIGHT, JEREMY, ed. *The letters of Bysshe and Timothy Shelley, and other documents from Horsham Museum & the West Sussex Record Office.* Horsham: Horsham Museum Society, 2000. 18-19th c. Includes 'calendar of documents relating to the Shelley family among the Hurst papers in the West Sussex Record Office'.

Stapley
TURNER, EDWARD. 'Extracts from the diary of Richard Stapley, gent, of Hickstead Place, in Twineham, from 1682' to 1724, with a notice of the Stapley family', *Sx.A.C.* **2**, 1849, 102-28. Includes pedigrees, 16-18th c.
TURNER, EDWARD. 'The Stapley diary', *Sx.A.C.* **18**, 1866, 151-62. Brief extracts, 18th c. Continuation of Richard Stapley's diary by his family.

Tompkins
EUSTACE, G.W. 'The Tompkins diary', *Sx.A.C.* **71**, 1930, 11-54. Family diary, 1768-1814.

Turner
TURNER, THOMAS. *The diary of Thomas Turner, 1754-1765,* ed. David Vaisey. Oxford: Oxford University Press, 1984. Includes pedigree of Turner, 18-19th c., and appendix on 'Principal persons figuring in the diary other than members of the diarist's immediate family'.

BLENCOWE, R.W., & LOWER, M.A. 'Extracts from the diary of a Sussex tradesman a hundred years ago', *Sx.A.C.* **11**, 1859, 179-220. Diary of Thomas Turner.

TURNER, THOMAS. *The diary of a Georgian shopkeeper: a selection ...,* ed. G.H. Jennings. 2nd ed. Oxford. Oxford University Press, 1979. Includes appendix: 'notes on family history written by Thomas Turner'.

TURNER, THOMAS. *Diary of Thomas Turner of East Hoathly (1754-1765),* ed. Florence Maris Turner. Bodley Head, 1925. Includes pedigree of Turner family 18th c., also notes on 'principal persons figuring in the diary'.

Unwin
See Cobden

Wilson
See Campion

5. FAMILY HISTORIES AND PEDIGREES

Abernon
MEEKINGS, C.A.F. 'Notes on the de Abernon family before 1236', *Sy.A.C.* **72**, 1980, 157-73. Includes pedigrees.

PERCEVAL, CHARLES SPENCER. 'Some account of the family of Abernon, of Albury and Stoke D'Abernon', *Sy.A.C.* **5**, 1871, 53-74. Medieval.

Acton
FORD, WYN F. 'The families of Acton of Ripe and Lulham of Hamsey', *Sx.F.H.* **6**(4), 1984, 137-9. 17th c.

Adsett
ADSETT, R. 'The Adsett family', *Petworth Society magazine* **66**, 1991, 21-5. Of Petworth, 18-19th c.

Aguillon
SALZMAN, L.F. 'The family of Aguillon', *Sx.A.C.* **79**, 1938, 45-60. Includes pedigree, 12-14th c.

Aiton
PAGNAMENTA, FRANK. 'The Aitons: gardeners to their majesties, and others', *R.H.* **18**, 1997, 7-19. 18th c.

Alard
SALZMAN, L.F. 'Some notes on the family of Alard', *Sx.A.C.* **61**, 1920, 126-41. See also **62**, 1921, 204-5. Includes 'skeleton pedigree', 13-15th c.

RHEDECYNIAN. 'Alard', *Notes and queries* **150**, 1926, 372-3. As witnesses in 13-14th c. charters.

Y., E. 'Alard', *Notes and queries* **158**, 1930, 60-61 & 78-9. See also 118. Extracts from 14th c. charters.

Alcock
See Blaxton

Alderslade
See Lanaway

Alexander
ADAMS, ROBERT. 'Alexander of Southwark, Surrey', *Blackmansbury* **4**(5 & 6), 1968, 133-7. 18-19th c.

Alford

POOLE, HELEN. 'The Alfords in Sussex', *Sussex history* **32**, 1991, 1-15. 17-18th c. *See also* Eversfield

Alfrey

LEPPARD, M.J. 'Recording the Alfreys of Gullege, East Grinstead', *Sx.F.H.* **6**(1), 1984, 22-4. 14-16th c.

Alphery

'Descendants of the Russian czars in Wandsworth', *Wandsworth notes and queries* **2**, 1898, 37-41. Alphery family, 17th c.

Apsley

COLLINGRIDGE, RUTH. 'Henry and Cordelia Apsley of Ticehurst, Co.Sussex', *Sx.N.Q.* **13**, 1950-53, 199-200. See also 244-7. 16-17th c.

Aquila

SHOOSMITH, EDWARD. 'Shadow of the eagle', *Sussex county magazine* **4**, 1929, 147-51. De Aquila family, 12-13th c.

Arnold

LANGHAM-CARTER, R.R. 'The Arnolds at Pains Hill Cottage', *Sy.A.C.* **69**, 1973, 169-74. In Street Cobham, 19th c.

Arrick

ARRICK, ANDREW. 'Arrick', *Notes & queries* **152**, 1927, 406, See also 447, & **153**, 1927, 359. Arrick family, 18-19th c.

Asbury

TAYLOR, ALAN. 'The Asbury family in the indexes of the Office of Population, Censuses and Surveys', *R. & B.* **4**(2), 1977, 58-63; **4**(3), 1978, 92-6; **4**(4), 1978, 115-9; **5**(1), 1978, 16-18; **5**(2), 1978, 50-52. Includes pedigrees, 19th c.

TAYLOR, ALAN. 'Is William my ancestor?' *R. & B.* **11**(4), 1985, 130-4. Asbury family of London, Southwark, *etc.,* 19th c.

Ashburnham

BURLINSON, MARK. 'The house of Ashburnham', *Battle & District Historical Society newsletter* **11**, 1992, 34-6. Brief lecture.

GUILMANT, AYLWIN. 'The ladies of Ashburnham', *Sx.G.L.H.* **7**(3 & 4), 1986, 95-104. 15-19th c.

SHOOSMITH, EDWARD. 'Which is the oldest Sussex family? The Ashburnhams', *Sussex county magazine* **16**, 1942, 329-30. Medieval.

Ashdown

See Newnham

Atherton

ATHERTON, RALPH S. 'Beyond the Workhouse: an Edwardian mystery', *Genealogists magazine* **17**, 1972-4, 261-5 & 604-10. Includes pedigrees of Atherton and Beard families, 19-20th c.

Aubertin

PRINGLE, CHARLES E. 'The Aubertins and Chipstead church windows', *L.H.R.* **13**, 1974, 9-12. 17-19th c.

Aubrey

BUTTREY, PAM. 'Aubrey's in Surrey', *E.Sy.F.H.S.J.* **12**(1), 1989, 22-3. 16-17th c.

Audley

'Audley of London and Rotherhithe' in READ, ALLEYNE LYELL. *Audley pedigrees.* Percy Lund Humphries & Co., 1926. 226-31. 17-18th c.

Austen

A[USTEN]-L[EIGH], R.A. *Pedigree of Austen, of Horsmonden, Broadford, Grovehurst, Kippington, Capel Manor, etc.* Spottiswoode, Ballantyne & Co., 1940. 16-20th c.

LAKIN, MARGARET. 'Some notes on Jane Austen's family connections with the villages of Danehill and Horsted Keynes', *D.P.H.S.M.* **2**(8), 1984, 18-24.

Awcock

LUCAS, P.G. 'Notes on Awcock of Chelworth', *D.P.H.S.M.* **5**(1), 1994, 16-17. Includes pedigree, 17-18th c.
'Awcock', *D.P.H.S.M.* **2**(7), 1984, 5-8. Includes pedigree, 19th c.

Aylwin

LEVER, R.A. 'The Aylwins of Treyford with Didling', *Sx.F.H.* **6**(5), 1984, 176-7. 18-19th c.

TROKE, R.C. 'The Aylwins', *Sx.N.Q.* **11**, 1946-7, 169-74. Medieval-18th c.

Aynscomb
'The Aynscombes of Mayfield', *Sx.G.L.H.* **1**(2), 1983, 76-8. 15-17th c.

Badlesmere
SNOWDEN, C.E. 'The De Baldesmeres of Bourne', *Sussex county magazine* **6**, 1932, 560-64. Includes pedigrees 12-14th c.
See also Clare

Baker
OSBORNE, B.E. 'The Bakers, brickmakers of Piddinghoe', *Sx.F.H.* **5**(2), 1982, 57-60. 18-19th c.
OSBORNE, B.E. 'The brickmaking Bakers of Piddinghoe', *Sx.G.L.H.* **3**(4), 1981, 127-9.
'Baker', *D.P.H.S.M.* **2**(7), 1984, 17-20. 18-19th c.
See also Osborne

Balchin
GREEN, PAT. 'The Balchins and Godalming', *R. & B.* **24**(3), 1997, 94-5. 17-20th c.
WOLFE, DARLEEN. 'It only takes a generation', *R & B.* **9**(1), 1982, 17-19. Balchin family, 19-20th c.

Baldy
CHALLEN, W.H. 'Baldy's Garden, the painters Lambert, and other Sussex families', *Sx.A.C.* **90**, 1952, 103-52. Baldy, Lambert Philcox, Duly, Beard, Smith, Chatfield and Winckton families, 17-18th c.; includes folded 'abridged pedigree of the painters James Lambert of Lewes, showing their connexions with the painters William, George and John Smith of Chichester', 18-19th c.

Baliol
FIELD, LAURENCE F. 'The Baliol family in Sussex, Normandy and Scotland', *Sx.N.Q.* **6**, 1936-7, 100-103. See also 158. Medieval.

Ballard
LINFIELD, MALCOLM. 'The Ballard family register', *W.Sx.H.* **58**, 1996, 10-13. 16-18th c.

Barclay
BARCLAY, CHARLES W., et al. *History of the Barclay family, with full pedigree from 1066 to [1933].* 3 vols. St. Catherine Press, 1924-34. Of Gloucestershire, Scotland, London, Walthamstow, Essex, and Bury Hill, Dorking.

Barentyne
WARD, FRANK. 'The divorce of Sir William Barentyne', *Sx.A.C.* **68**, 1927, 279-81. 16th c.

Barham
FITZGERALD-UNIACKE, R.G. 'The Barhams of Shoesmiths in Wadhurst', *Sx.A.C.* **56**, 1914, 110-60. 13-18th c.

Barnard
COLLINS, RICHARD. 'Another later marriage', *Sx.F.H.* **13**(4), 1998, 141-3. Barnard family, 18th c.

Barnes
CLEMENTS, RUTH. 'A family tale', *H. & R.F.H.S.J.* **6**(1), 1991, 4-8. Barnes family, 19th c.

Barrantyne
BUDGEN WALTER. 'The divorce of Sir Wm. Barrantyne, 1540', *Sx.N.Q.* **9**, 1942-3, 168-70.

Barraud
BARRAUD, E.M. 'The Barraud family of Lambeth', *Lambethan quarterly* **11**, 1966, 13. 18-20th c.

Bartelot
BARTELOT, R. GROSVENOR. 'Bartelot of Ernley', *Sx.N.Q.* **7**, 1938-9, 76-8. 16-17th c.

Baster
NOBLE, JEAN C. 'A photographic mystery story', *Family tree magazine* **10**(3), 1994, 21-3. Baster family, 18-19th c.; of London, Essex and Surrey.

Bateman
BATEMAN, ROGER. *Bateman family history (Folkestone and, later, Sussex).* 6 fiche. Kent Family History Society record publication **1064**. 1988. Includes pedigree, 16-20th c.

BATEMAN, ROGER. 'Born losers: an irreverent look at ancestry', *Kent Family History Society journal* **7**(6), 1994, 204-6. Bateman family of Folkestone and Bermondsey; includes pedigree, 16-20th c.

Battelle

BATTELLE, LUCY. *A history of the Battelle family in England*. Columbus: Battelle Press, 1985. Includes chapter on 'The Ewell family, Surrey', and 'the families connected with Sussex'. Extensive; primarily of Essex and Suffolk, etc.

Bax

THISTLETHWAITE, BERNARD. *The Bax family: an account of the early Quaker Baxes of Capel and Ockley in the County of Surrey, with particulars of some of their descendants and notes relating to a number of allied families*. Headley Brothers, 1936. 17-19th c., includes pedigrees of Bax, Kidd, Prichard, Payne, Tulley and Holmes. Extensive.

Baynes

CARTER, HILARY. 'The Baynes family of Fitzwalters, St. Johns Road', *E.L.H.* **107**, 1998, 6-8. In Eastbourne. 19-20th c.

Beams

THOMPSON, PETER. 'A family tragedy', *E.Sy.F.H.S.J.* **19**(4), 1996, 35-6. Beams family of Ewell, 18-19th c.

Beard

See Atherton and Baldy

Beaufoy

GUNASENA, DIANA. 'The Beaufoys at Battersea', *Wandsworth historian* **61**, 1990, 1-8 & 22; **64**, 1992, 1-4; **68**, 1997, 1-7. Includes pedigree, 17-20th c.
KERR, BARBARA. 'The Beaufoys of Lambeth', *History today* **23**, 1973, 495-502. 18-19th c.

Beazley

BEAZLEY, F.C. *Pedigree of the family of Beazley*. Mitchell Hughes & Clarke, 1921. Of Alverstoke, Hampshire, Kenley and Wallington, Surrey and Oxton, Cheshire, 18-20th c.

Beckford

GOLLIN, G.J. 'The Beckford family and Ashtead', *P.L.D.L.H.S.* **4**(5), 1981, 134-40. Includes pedigree, 17-18th c.

Beldham

GOODALL, DARYL. 'Discovering Beldham', *E.Sy.F.H.S.J.* **13**(2), 1990, 16-17; **13**(3), 1990, 14-17. Beldham family, 19th c.

Bellingham

FOLJAMBE, CECIL G. SAVILE. 'Extracts from the parish registers of Newtimber, Sussex, relating to the families of Bellingham and Woodcock', *Sx.A.C.* **38**, 1892, 206-9. 16-17th c.

Benn(e)

'Benne pedigree', *M.G.H.* 2nd series **1**, 1886, 140-43 & 157. Of London and Surrey, 16-17th c.; includes monumental inscriptions, will of Sir Anthony Benn, 1618, and extracts from registers of Kingston on Thames.

Bennett

BENNETT, JUNE. 'The Bennett family of Lymington, Farnham and Basingstoke', *Hampshire family historian* **8**(2), 1986, 107-10. 19th c.
'Bennett the broom makers', *D.P.H.S.M.* **2**(7), 1984, 9-11. 16-19th c.

Bentley

MCCANN, TIMOTHY J. 'Catherine Bentley, great grand-daughter of St Thomas More, and her Catholic connections in Sussex', *Moreana* **11**, 1974, 41-5. 17th c.

Berchard

BOXALL, K. 'Calling all Berchards/Birchards', *Sx.F.H.* **14**(1), 2000, 25-6. Pedigree, 19th c.

Best

GOULD, D. 'W. Best & Son, coal merchants', *Bulletin of the East Grinstead Society* **38**, 1985, 7-9. Best family, 19-20th c.

Bethell

BETHEL, DAVID 'In search of James Bethell, an artist working from 1827 to 1835', *E.Sy.F.H.S.J.* **16**(3), 1993, 23-7. Includes pedigree, 18-19th c.

Bettesworth
CHATTERTON-NEWMAN, ROGER. 'The Bettesworths: a West Sussex dynasty', *W.Sx.H.* **53**, 1994, 15-18. 16-19th c.

Bevington
BEVINGTON, GEOFFREY. *Bevington & Sons, Bermondsey 1795-1950: a chronicle.* [The author], 1993. History of a family firm.

Bicknell
BICKNELL, A. SIDNEY. *Five generations: Bicknell of Taunton; Bicknell of Bridgwater; Bicknell of Farnham; Browne (Le Brune) of France and Spitalfields; Wilde of High Wycombe.* George Sherwood, 1912. Medieval-19th c.; includes pedigrees.

Bignold
BIGNOLD, ROBERT, SIR. *Five generations of the Bignold family, 1761-1947, and their connection with the Norwich Union.* B.T.Batsford, 1948. Originally of Surrey, subsequently of Norfolk. Includes pedigree, 14-20th c.

Bilson
CHALLEN, WILLIAM HAROLD. 'Thomas Bilson, Bishop of Winchester, his family, and their Hampshire, Sussex, and other connections', *Hampshire Field Club & Archaeological Society papers and proceedings* **19**(1), 1955, 35-46; **19**(3), 1957, 253-75.

Bine
See Byne

Bingham
CRESSWELL, FRANK. 'John Bingham of Southwark, squire saddler to Queen Elizabeth and James I', *E.Sy.F.H.S.J.* **17**(3), 40-42.

Birchard
See Berchard

Blake
MOZLEY, GERALDINE. *The Blakes of Rotherhithe.* Privately printed, 1935. Includes pedigree, 17-19th c.

Blaker
RENSHAW, W.C. *Searches into the history of the family of Blaker of Sussex.* Rev.ed. Chiswick Press, 1904. Medieval-19th c.; includes folded pedigree. 40 copies only printed.

Blaxton
CHALLEN, W.H. 'Henry Blaxton, D.D.', *Sx.N.Q.* **14**, 1954-7, 221-5. See also **15**, 1958-62, 31. 16-17th c.

JENKINS, PETER R. 'Some clerical dynasties in early seventeenth century Sussex', *Sussex history* 2(3), 1982, 16-19. Brief study of the Blaxton, Alcock, and Frewen families, *etc.*

Bludworth
BASTIAN, F. 'Leatherhead families of the 16th and 17th centuries, VI. Bludworth of Thorncroft', *P.L.D.L.H.S.* 2(6), 1962, 177-86. Includes pedigree.

Blunt
BLENCOWE, R.W. 'The Blunt family', *Sx.A.C.* **13**, 1861, 311-12. Brief note on families of Blunt and Scawen, 17-18th c.

BLUNT, REGINALD. *Memoirs of Gerald Blunt of Chelsea, his family and forbears.* Truslove & Hanson, 1911. Includes folded pedigree of Blunt of Sussex, medieval-20th c.

Board
See Boord

Bohun
SNOWDEN, CHARLES EDMUND. 'The de Bohuns of Midhurst', *Sussex county magazine* **7**, 1933, 307-13. Includes pedigrees, 12-16th c.

WATSON, G.W. 'The Bohuns of Midhurst', *Genealogist* N.S. **28**, 1912, 1-16, 114-23 & 173-4. 11-16th c.
See also Braose

Bolingbroke
SMALLWOOD, FRANK THEODORE. 'Bolingbroke's birthplace', *Wiltshire archaeological and natural history magazine* **60**, 1965, 96-9. Rival claims of Lydiard Tregoze, Wiltshire, and Battersea.

Bond
TURNER, FREDERIC. 'Notes on some Surrey pedigrees', *Sy.A.C.* **30**, 1917, 1-12. Includes pedigree of Bond and Denham, 16-17th c.

Bonville
COOPER, WILLIAM DURRANT. 'The Bonvilles of Halnaker', *Sx.A.C.* **15**, 1863, 57-66. Medieval; includes wills of John Bonville, 1494, and Katherine Bonville, 1497.

Bonwicke
BAX, ALFRED RIDLEY. 'On a ledger to the memory of James Bonwicke, esq., in Mickleham churchyard, Surrey, with some account of the Bonwicke family', *Sy.A.C.* **13**, 1897, 111-29. Includes folded pedigree, 17-18th c., and several wills.

Booker
MAY, EVE. 'Booker Brothers: builders of Bognor', *B.R.L.H.S.N.* **23**, 1990, 23-5. 18-20th c.
See also Bowker

Boord
LOWER, MARK ANTONY. 'Memoranda relating to the family of Boord, Borde, or Board', *Sx.A.C.* **6**, 1853, 197-214. Includes pedigree, 17-19th c.

Booth
PELLETT, MARY. 'James Booth', *H. & R.F.H.S.* **15**(1), 2000, 5-12. 19th c. Booth family.

Borde
COOPER, J.H. 'Old Cuckfield families', *Sx.A.C.* **41**, 1898, 203-15. See also **42**, 1899, 244-6; **43**, 1900, 279-80. Borde family, 16-18th c.
See also Boord

Borel
COOPER, J.H. 'Cuckfield families, III', *Sx.A.C.* **43**, 1900, 1-43. Borel or Burrell family, 15-19th c. Includes folded pedigrees.

Bosher
DAVIS, DOROTHY. 'The Bosher family of Egham', *R. & B.* **25**(1), 1998, 8-9; **25**(2), 1998, 56-7; **26**(2), 1999, 67-8. 19th c.

Boteler
See De Mara

Botting
BURCHALL, MICHAEL. 'A Brighton celebrity: James Botting the executioner', *Sx.F.H.* **14**(1), 2000, 5-11. 18-19th c.
'Botting', *D.P.H.S.M.* **2**(7), 1984, 12-13. 19th c.

Boughton
MOLYNEAUX-CHILD, JOHN. 'The Boughtons: the rise of a yeoman family', *Send & Ripley History Society newsletter* **62**, 1985, 2. Brief note, 16-19th c.

Boulton
CLUBE, J.R. 'The Boulton family of Thorncroft Manor 1763-1828', *P.L.D.L.H.S.* **6**(1), 1997, 10-13.

Bourn
EVERSHED, P.B. 'Bourn of Keymer: an incomplete family history', *Sx.F.H.* **8**(3), 1988, 99. 18th c.

Bowelly
See Bullie

Bowker
'Notes as to family of Bowker or Booker: extracts from the church registers of Horsham, Sussex', *M.G.H.* 2nd series **3**, 1890, 397-8. 16-17th c.

Bowyer
BOWYER, PERCY A. 'Notes concerning the Bowyer family', *Sx.A.C.* **64**, 1923, 105-8. Includes pedigrees, 16th c.
COOPER, J.H. 'Cuckfield families', *Sx.A.C.* **42**, 1899, 19-53. See also **43**, 1900, 279-80. Bowyer family; includes folded pedigree, 16-17th c.
NICHOLS, JOHN GOUGH. 'Bowyer of Camberwell', *Sy.A.C.* **3**, 1865, 220-26. 16-17th c.
PATCHING, JOHN. 'Sir Thomas Bowyer, Bart., M.P. for Bramber, and his family', *Sx.A.C.* **45**, 1902, 209-11. Includes pedigree of Bowyer of Leythorne, 16-17th c.

Box
ELLIS, W.S. 'Notes on the family of Box', *Genealogist* **1**, 1877, 97-100. Of Kent and Sussex; includes wills, extracts from parish registers, *etc.*

Boxall
PELLING, GEORGE. 'Memories of Aunt Bess', *Sx.F.H.* **3**(7), 1978, 198-203. Boxall family, 18-20th c; includes pedigrees shewing relationship to Hawkins, Passifull, *etc.*

Bradbury
See Whitgift

Bradford
MUNCEY, FRANCES. 'Bradfords the coal merchants', *E.L.H.* **115**, 2000, 12-16. 19-20th c.

Bradshaw
See Drew

Braman
CHALLEN, W.H. 'John Braman of Chichester and Lewes', *Sx.N.Q.* **15**, 1958-62, 32-3. 17-18th c.
GODFREY, WALTER H. 'John Braman of Chichester and Lewes: a second marriage', *Sx.A.C.* **69**, 1928, 228-9. Early 18th c.

Braose
COOPER, WILLIAM DURRANT. 'The families of Braose of Chesworth, and Hoo', *Sx.A.C.* **8**, 1856, 97-131. Includes pedigree of Braose, 13-14th c. and Hoo, 11-15th c. Challenged in HOO, HAMILTON. 'Pedigree of Hoo', *Sx.A.C.* **45**, 1902, 186-97.
ELWES, DUDLEY GEORGE CARY. *The family of De Braose, 1066-1326.* Exeter: William Pollard, 1883.
ELWES, DUDLEY G. CARY. 'De Braose family', *Genealogist* **4**, 1880, 133-41 & 235-44; **5**, 1881, 65-70, 161-7 & 318-25; **6**, 1882, 236-47; **7**, 1883, 51-60. Medieval; includes pedigree of Bohun of Midhurst.
GRANTHAM, T. 'History notices of Bramber Castle, and of the family of De Braose', *Sx.A.C.* **5**, 1852, 147-54. Medieval.

Brassey
HAINES, PAMELA. 'The Brasseys of Normanhurst', *Battle and District Historical Society newsletter* **12**, 1993, 22-5. 19-20th c.

Bray
BRANDON, P.F. 'A twentieth century squire in his landscape', *Southern history* **4**, 1982, 191-220. Bray family of Shere, with brief notes, 15-20th c.

'The Brays of Shere', *Ancestor* **6**, 1903, 1-10. 15-19th c.

Brocas
BURROWS, MONTAGU. *The family of Brocas of Beaurepaire and Roche Court, hereditary masters of the royal buckhounds* ... Longmans Green and Co., 1886. Medieval-19th c., includes folded pedigree, with abstracts of 462 deeds relating to Hampshire, Berkshire, Surrey and Yorkshire, etc.

Brodie
LEWIS, M. 'Brodie family', *E.L.H.S.N.* **33-4**, 1979, 6-8. 18-19th c.

Brodrick
ENSING, RITA J. 'Dunsford Manor and the Brodrick family in Wandsworth', *Wandsworth historian* **42**, 1984, 15-22; **44**, 1985, 8-14. Includes pedigree, 16-19th c.
MIDLETON, VISCOUNT. 'Brodrick genealogy', *M.G.H.* **2**, 1876, 359-70. Of Yorkshire, Surrey, etc., medieval-19th c.
SCHOMBERG, ARTHUR. 'Brodrick', *M.G.H.* 4th series **3**, 1910, 137-9. Includes will of Sir Allen Brodrick of Wandsworth, 1680.

Brooman
BROOMAN, RONALD C. 'Notes on the Brooman family of East Sussex', *H. & R.F.H.S.J.* **3**(3), 1988, 52-5. See also **6**(2), 1991, 34. 19th c., includes pedigree, 18th c.

Brown(e)
MILLS, SUE. 'The Browns of Reigate', *E.Sy.F.H.S.J.* **20**(1), 1997, 32-3. 19th c.
'Browne and Lee family extracts from the parish register of Rusper, Co. Sussex, England', *New England historical and genealogical register* **61**, 1907, 116-8. 16-17th c.
See also Bicknell

Brownrigg
See Davies

Buckle
RICE, ROBERT GARROWAY. 'The Buckles of Banstead, Co.Surrey', *Genealogist* **3**, 1879, 251-8. Includes extracts from parish registers, 17-19th c.

Budge
GERHOLD, PETER. 'The 'Retreat' and the Budge family', *Wandsworth historian* **64**, 1992, 14-16. 18-19th c., on Upper Richmond Road.

Budgen
DAVIS, RON. 'Budgen: a trading family', *Surrey history* **5**(1), 1994, 25-45. Includes pedigrees, 18-19th c.
FINCH, PETER. 'The Budgen family of Nutfield', *L.H.R.* **26**, 1987, 16-20. 15-19th c.

Bull
SALZMAN, L.F. 'The Bulls of Sussex', *Sx.A.C.* **63**, 1922, 113-56. Medieval-19th c.

Bullen
FRANKLYN, CHARLES A.H. *The genealogy of Anne the Queen (Anne Bullen) and other English families ...* [ ]: privately printed, 1977. The 'other English families' covered includes Walwyn of Kilmersdon and Frome, Somerset, and of Bognor Regis.

Bullie
BURCHALL, MICHAEL J. 'Aliases', *Sx.F.H.* **3**(7), 1978, 214-5. Includes pedigree of Bullie or Bowelly, als Jordan, 16-17th c.

Burder
MERSON, R.A. 'The Burder family at Tilford House in the 1830's', *F.M.S.Q.N.* **6**(1), 1981, 29-33. See also **6**(5), 1982, 111-12; **6**(7), 1982, 153-4.

Burgess
BAYNE, KIM. 'Burgess family, wheelwrights', *Sx.F.H.* **6**(2), 1984, 53-4. 18-20th c.
BURGESS, DON. 'Ancestral immobility', *Sx.F.H.* **9**(3), 1990, 103-4. Burgess family of Hellingly, 17-18th c.
BURGESS, DON. 'The Burgesses of Brighton', *Sx.F.H.* **12**(1), 1996, 34-8. 19th c.
BURGESS, THOMAS. 'Thomas Burgess in Ewhurst parish (1773-1835)', *Sx.F.H.* **13**(1), 1998, 3-4. 19th c.

Burkin
WILTSHIRE, ELAINE. 'The Burkin family', *E.Sy.F.H.S.J.* **3**(1), 1980, 10-12 & 28. Of Surrey, Kent, London, *etc.*, general discussion of a one-name study.

Burn(s)
SMITH, RICHARD J. 'The benevolent Burns of Richmond Hill', *R.H.* **18**, 1997, 53-5. 18-19th c.
See also Spooner

Burrell
See Borel

Burtenshaw
BEAR, MARY. *Some Sussex Burtenshaws 1560-1991: Bolney, Alfriston, Clayton, Ditchling, Plumpton, Darenth (Kent), Hailsham, and overseas: one family of many in the county.* Eastbourne: the author, 1991. Includes pedigrees, 17-20th c.

Byne
RENSHAW, WALTER C. 'The Bynes of Rowdell, in Washington, Co. Sussex', *Genealogist* N.S. **23**, 1907, 1-11. 16-18th c.
RENSHAW, WALTER CHARLES *Searches into the history of the family of Byne or Bine of Sussex.* [2nd ed]. Chiswick Press, 1913. 35 copies only printed. Medieval-19th c.; includes folded pedigrees.
RENSHAW, WALTER C. 'The Bynes of Carshalton, Co.Surrey', *Genealogist* N.S. **23**, 1907, 213-9. 17-19th c.

Byron
ELLIS, D.B. 'The Byrons of Leatherhead', *P.L.D.L.H.S.* **5**(6), 1993, 161-3. Includes pedigree, 17-19th c.

Caesar
ELLMORE, MARY. 'The Caesar connection', *Longshot: journal of the Lin(d)field One Name Group* **4**(1), 1995, 13-19; **5**(1), 1996, 11-21. Includes pedigrees of Caesar, 18-20th c.

Campion
GREEN, EVERARD. 'Pedigree of Campion of Campions Hall, Co. Essex, of Combwell, Co.Kent, and of Danny, Co. Sussex', *M.G.H.* 4th series **2**, 1908, 261-7. 16-20th c.

Cantlowe
PLOMER, H.R. 'Some notes about the Cantlowe family', *Home counties magazine* **6**, 1904, 42-7. Of Streatham, 15th c.

Carew

MICHELL, RONALD. *The Carews of Beddington*. London Borough of Sutton Libraries and Arts Services, 1981. Includes pedigree, 15-19th c.

'Carew of Beddington', *Sy.A.C.* 1, 1858, 240-41. Pedigree, medieval-17th c.

See also Saunder

Caroline

SPENCER, WILLIAM E. 'Caroline complications', *E.Sy.F.H.S.J.* 17(2), 1994, 41-5. Caroline family of South London, *etc.*, 19th c.

SPENCER, WILLIAM E. 'Caroline news', *E.Sy.F.H.S.J.* 18(1), 1995, 31-5. Of Deptford and Canada, 19th c.

SPENCER, WILLIAM E. 'Her name was Caroline', *E.Sy.F.H.S.J.* 15(3), 1992, 11-18. Caroline family of South London, 19th c.

Carrill

Four families in Wonersh and Bramley. Wonersh: Wonersh History Society, 1997. Brief histories of the families of Carrill, Norton (later Grantley), Sparkes and Courage.

Carter

KIDD, SUE. 'My Bognor ancestors', *B.R.L.H.S.N.* 36, 1997, 25-28. Carter family, 18-20th c.

Caryll

ARNOLD, H.E.B. 'Caryll: an extinct Sussex family', *Sussex county magazine* 12, 1938, 397-401, 454-60, & 544-9. Includes pedigrees, 15-18th c.

DE TRENQUALÉON, MAX. *West-Grinstead et les Caryll: etudes historique et religieuse sur le comte de Sussex in Angleterre.* Paris: Chez M.Torré, 1893. Caryll family, medieval-18th c. In French.

HERNAMAN, IRENE. 'Carylls of West Sussex', *Sussex county magazie* 2, 1928, 302-5. 16-17th c.

HICKMAN, DENIS. 'The Caryll family and hunted priests', *Sussex county magazine* 19, 1945, 97-9. 16-18th c.

Cawley

ARNOLD, FREDERICK H. 'Cawley the Regicide', *Sx.A.C.* 34, 1886, 21-38. Includes pedigree, 17th c.

Challen

CHALLEN, W.H. 'Crypt Farm, Cocking', *Sx.N.Q.* 16, 1963-7, 49-52. Descent in the Challen family, 16-19th c.

Chaloner

ATTREE, F.W.T. 'Notes on the family of Chaloner of Cuckfield', *Sx.A.C.* 44, 1901, 116-39. Includes folded pedigree, 15-17th c.; also wills of Margaret Turner, 1618 and of various Chaloner family members.

Chamberlain

CHAMBERLAIN, JOAN. 'By any other name', *West Middlesex Family History Society journal* 3(4), 1983, 91-3. Chamberlain family of London and Richmond; includes pedigree, 18-20th c.

Chandler

CHANDLER, BETTY M. 'Bounty immigrants'. *Sx.F.H.* 9(1), 1990, 29-30. Chandler family of Lewes, migrants to Sydney; includes pedigree, 18-19th c.

Chapman

See Marchant

Charlesworth

HUGHES, JOHN. 'Finding Vernon John Charlesworth's children', *Cockney ancestor: the journal of the East of London Family History Society* 69, 1995-6, 46-8. In Lambeth, Stockwell, etc., 19th c.

Chatfield

FRENCH, ELIZABETH. 'Genealogical research in England: Chatfield' *New England historical and genealogical register* 70, 1916, 55-65 & 125-36. Chatfield family of Chichester; includes wills, parish register and lay subsidy extracts, deeds etc, medieval-17th c.

PIPER, D.J.W. 'Henry Chatfield', *Sx.N.Q.* 16, 1963-7, 16-19. Several members of the family were rectors of Balcombe between 1693 and 1818.

TYLER, J.C. 'Chatfield', *M.G.H.* 5th series 6, 1926-8, 195-8. Pedigree, 16-19th c., with wills.

See also Baldy

Chatterton

CHATTERTON-NEWMAN, ROGER. 'His curse ... is God's blessing', *W.Sx.H.* **54,** 1994, 19-21. Chatterton family, late 16th c.

Chaworth

'Chaworth and Kniveton family alliance', *Reliquary* **22,** 1881-2, 126. Of Surrey and Derbyshire, 17th c.

Chesney

SALZMAN, L.F. 'Sussex Domesday tenants, IV: the family of Chesney or Cheyney', *Sx.A.C.* **65,** 1924, 20-53. See also **66,** 1925, 236-7. Includes folded pedigrees, 11-17th c.

Cheynell

KEAN, GRAHAM, & KETTEMAN, TONY. 'The Cheynells, father and son: a crazy hedge divine ... and well principled gent', *W.Sx.H.* **58,** 1996, 18-30. 17-18th c.

Cheyney

See Chesney

Child

CHILD, KENNETH. *Some account of the Child family, 1550-1861.* Chichester: Phillimore, 1973. Of Kent and Sussex; includes pedigree, 16-20th c.

Chitty

CHITTY, ERIK. 'Chitty of Godalming', *R. & B.* **1**(4), 1975, 130-33. 14-18th c.

C., H. 'Note to Manning and Bray's *History of Surrey.* vol.II, page 43: Elizabeth Chitty', *Sy.A.C.* **15,** 1900, 160. Brief note on Chitty of Witley, early 18th c.

CHITTY, ERIK. 'Chitty of Chiltley?' *Family history journal of the South-East Hampshire Genealogical Society* **1**(4), 1974, 81-2. Includes pedigree of Chitty of Hampshire and Surrey, 16-17th c.

Chownes

RENSHAW, WALTER C. 'The Chownes of Alfriston, Co.Sussex', *Genealogist* N.S. **24,** 1908, 73-80. 16-18th c.

Christmas

KIRBY, EILEEN. 'Martha Chris(t)mas', *H. & R.F.H.S.J.* **10**(3), 1995, 50-51. 19th c.

Churcher

See Zillwood

Clare

HODSOLL, VERA. 'Bartholomew de Badlesmere', *E.L.H.S.N.* **40,** 1981, 5-8; **41,** 1981, 9-10; **42,** 1981, 4-6. Brief note on the medieval families of Clare and Badlesmere.

MALDEN, HENRY ELLIOT. 'Blechingley Castle and the De Clares', *Sy.A.C.* **15,** 1900, 17-26. Medieval.

Clarke

WRIGHT, SIMON. 'A remarkable Sussex family', *Hindsight: the journal of the Uckfield & District Preservation Society* **1,** 1995, 36-9. Clarke family; includes pedigrees, 17-18th c.

Clarkson

WRIGHT, MICHAEL. 'Queen Victoria's little wars: the Clarkson family', *R. & B.* **26**(4), 2000, 161-3. Of Kingston on Thames, St. Pancras, *etc.* 19-20th c.

Cleaver

See Delves

Clive

WALKER, T.E.C. 'The Clives at Claremont', *Sy.A.C.* **65,** 1968, 91-6. Late 18th c.

Clowes

CLOWES, W.B. *Family business 1803-1953.* William Clowes and Sons, [1953?] Of Chichester and London, includes pedigree, 16-20th c.

Cobden

PRITCHARD, ELEANOR. *Cobden country.* [ ]: Midhurst Society, 1981. Brief history of Cobden family, 19th c.

PRITCHARD, ELEANOR. 'The daughters of Cobden', *W.Sx.H.* **25,** 1983, 17-23; **26,** 1983, 27-31. 19th c.

WADDAMS, MARGARET. 'The Cobden family of West Sussex: a search for personalities', *Sx.F.H.* **8**(1), 1988, 3-8. Includes pedigrees, 18th c.

WADDAMS, MARGERY. 'The Newland case, or things being in great confusion', *Sx.F.H.* **13**(7), 1999, 236-40. Cobden and Newland families, 17-18th c.

WADDAMS, MARGERY. 'The Reverend Edward Cobden, M.A., D.D., (1683-1764)', *Sx.F.H.* 8(8), 1989, 345-8. Includes pedigree, 17-18th c.

Cobham
FLOWER, JOHN WICKHAM. 'Notices of the family of Cobham of Sterborough Castle, Lingfield, Surrey', *Sy.A.C.* 2, 1864, 115-94. Medieval; includes pedigree, 13-15th c., and wills, *etc.*

P[ERCEVAL], C.S., & F[LOWER], J.W. 'Memorandum on the notices of the family of Cobham of Sterborough', *Sy.A.C.* 2, 1864, 224-6.

Cole(s)
COLE, JAMES EDWIN. *The genealogy of the family of Cole, of the County of Devon, and of those of its branches which settled in Suffolk, Hampshire, Surrey, Lincolnshire and Ireland.* J.R.Smith, 1867. Medieval-19th c.'

'Short record of John Henry Campion Coles & Sons, solicitors', *E.L.H.S.N.* 81, 1991, 27-9. Coles family, 19th c.

Colepeper
ATTREE, F.W.T., & BOOKER, J.H.L. 'The Sussex Colepepers', *Sx.A.C.* 47, 1904, 47-81; 48, 1905, 65-98. Includes folded pedigrees of Colepeper of Wigsell and Hollingbourne, 16-20th c. Colepeper of Aylesford, 14-18th c., Culpeper of Barbados, 17-20th c., and Culpeper of Wakehurst, 16-17th c.

Colgate
FERGUSON, PETER. 'The Colgates at Bridge Cottage, Uckfield: the story of an eighteenth century farmhouse', *Sx.F.H.* 7(1), 1986, 3-5. 18th c.

Collins
ETTRIDGE, ROBERT B. 'Any more for the Skylark?! Captain Fred Collins of Brighton', *Sx.F.H.* 5, 1982, 17-25 & 42-5. Includes pedigrees of Collins shewing relationship to Shepherd and Ettridge, 19-20th c., also of Gillam, 18-20th c.

UNIACKE, R.G.FITZGERALD. 'Collins of New England', *Sx.N.Q.* 3, 1931, 225 & 257-8. 17th c.

Collyer
PUGH, PAMELA. 'Hill Place and the Collyer family', *R. & B.* 10(3), 1983, 92-5. At Knaphill; 17-19th c.

Colwell
COLWELL, MORRIS A. 'The Colwells of East Dean', *Sx.F.H.* 10(6), 1993, 233-6. Includes pedigree, 18-19th c.

Comber
BARROW, GEOFFREY B. *The Comber family, with notes on the various families of the surname Rivers.* Research Publishing, 1980. Includes folded pedigrees, 16-19th c.; of Sussex, Surrey, and Yorkshire.

COMBER, JOHN. 'The Combers of Shermanbury, Chichester and Allington', *Sx.A.C.* 49, 1906, 128-56. Includes folded pedigree, 16-17th c.

COMBER, JOHN. 'The family of Comber of Wotton', *Genealogists magazine* 6, 1932-4, 129-40. Of Surrey and Sussex, 17-18th c.

Comfort/Comport
See Cornford

Constable
KENDELL, MOYA. 'Constables in Sussex', *W.Sx.H.* 44, 1989, 26-9. Constable family, 19th c.

Cooper
HEWITT, MAURICE. 'Serendipity and the chance discovery of unsuspected local history', *F.M.S.Q.N.* 9(5), 1991, 79-82. Cooper and Hammond families, 19th c., includes Hammond pedigree, 18th c.

Copper
COPPER, BOB. *A song for every season: a hundred years of a Sussex farming family.* New ed. Peacehaven: Coppersongs, 1997. Copper family, 19-20th c.

Copley
SANBORN, V.C. 'The Copleys of Roughey and Gatton', *Genealogist* N.S., 33, 1917, 73-80. Includes pedigrees, 15-16th c.

Coppin
COPPIN, TONY. 'The Coppin family of Addington', *E.Sy.F.H.S.J.* 14(1), 1991, 7-9. 18th c.

Cornford

CORNFORD, JOHN. 'Tracing a name: the origins of the Cornford, Comport and Comfort family names', *North West Kent family history* **4**(10), 1988, 376-84. In East Sussex and West Kent.

Cottee

BUSHELL, VALERIE. 'The Cottee family of Ewell, Surrey', *E.Sy.F.H.S.J.* **18**(3), 1995, 19-24. 18-19th c.

Cottee

BUSHELL, VALERIE. 'The Cottee family of Ewell, Surrey', *The Peeler* **1**, 1996, 39-40.

Cotton

EXWOOD, MAURICE. 'William Cotton and his family', *P.L.D.L.H.S.* **5**(6), 1993, 163-70. Includes pedigree, 18-19th c.

Coulthurst

BROWN, JOHN W. *The Coulthursts of Streatham Lodge.* Streatham: Local History Publications, 1993. Includes 'pedigree of Coulthurst of Gargrave', 17-19th c. The family moved to Streatham in 1836.

Courage

See Carrill

Courthope

'Ancient deeds in illustration of the descent of the Courthopes, of Goudhurst, Co.Kent, and Wyleigh, Co.Sussex', *Collectanea topographica et genealogica* **2**, 1835, 393-8.

Coussmaker

ASHWORTH, PAT. & KINDER, JACK. *Westwood, Normandy: the story of a Surrey elite.* Guildford: Westwood Place Management, 1998. Coussmaker family, 17-20th c., includes pedigree.

Covert

COOPER, J.H. 'The Coverts', *Sx.A.C.* **46**, 1903, 170-80; **47**, 1904, 116-47; **48**, 1905, 1-15. See also **48**, 1905, 150-51. Includes pedigree of 'Covert of Chaldon, Sullington and Slaugham', 13-18th c.

Cranmer

WATERS, ROBERT EDMOND CHESTER. *Genealogical memoirs of the kindred families of Thomas Cranmer, Archbishop of Canterbury, and Thomas Wood, Bishop of Lichfield, illustrated with twelve short pedigrees, engravings of all Archbishop Cranmer's official shields, and shields of arms.* Robson and Sons, 1877. Cranmer of Mitcham, Surrey, Aslacton, Norfolk, Astwoodbury, Buckinghamshire, and Loudham, Suffolk. Wood of Hackney, Kensington and Suffolk. Includes pedigrees, 15-16th c.

Crawford/Crawfurd

CRAWFURD, G.P. 'The family of Crawfurd in Scotland and Sussex', *Scottish notes and queries* 3rd series **4**, 1926, 125-8, 161-5, 179-82, 200-202 & 217-9. 17-19th c.

PACKHAM, ROGER. 'The Crawfords of Cane Hill', *L.H.R.* **13**, 1974, 10-14. 19-20th c.

CRAWFURD, G.P. 'Crawfurd of Ardmillan, Ayrshire, and of East Grinstead and Lindfield, Co.Sussex', *M.G.H.* 5th series **6**, 1926-8, 3-8. 16-20th c.

PACKHAM, R. 'The sweet harmony of the Crawfords', *L.H.R.* **18**, 1979, 30-31. 19-20th c.

Cree

MACKENZIE, BERYL. 'The Cree nursery at Addlestone', *Surrey history* **3**(4), 1987/8, 165-75. Includes notes on the Cree family, 18-19th c.

Creuze

'Refugee families: Creuze of Essex and Surrey', *Herald and genealogist* **1**, 1863, 259-61. 18-19th c.

Creffield

ROUND, J.H. 'The Creffield family', *Genealogist* N.S., **3**, 1898, 80-83. Of London and Surrey; includes pedigree, 18th c.

Cricketot

See Poynings

Cromwell

PHILLIPS, JOHN. 'Cromwells of Putney', *Antiquarian magazine and bibliographer* **2**, 1882, 56-62 & 178-86; **5**, 1884, 171-9. 15-16th c.

Crowhurst
BUTTON, PAT. 'Six James Crowhursts - five too many!' *Sx.F.H.* **8**(7), 1989, 328-9. Includes pedigrees, 18-19th c.
COUPER, GILLIAN M. 'Stones that tell a story, 3', *F.R.* **10**(3), 1996, 67. Notes on the Crowhurst family of Wilmington, 18th c.

Cruttenden
See Eldridge

Culpeper
MCLEAN, DAVID. 'Sussex and the U.S.A., second series no.l: Sussex and the Culpepers', *Sussex county magazine* **5**, 1931, 24-30. 16-17th c.
'John Culpeper', *Sx.N.Q.* **3**, 1931, 28. Note on a marriage of 1611.
See also Colepeper

Cummings
'In search of Mrs [and Mr.] Cummings', *Petworth Society magazine* **83**, 1996, 18-23. Late 19th c. Petworth family.

Dabner
DABNER, R.J. 'The children of Ephraim', *R. & B.* **2**(4), 1976, 147-50; **3**(1), 1976, 9-13; **3**(2) 1976, 50-5. Dabner family, 16-19th c.

Dacres
See Godman

Dallaway
STEER, FRANCIS W. 'Memoir and letters of James Dallaway; 1763-1834', *Sx.A.C.* **103**, 1965, 1-48. See also **105**, 1967, 62-9. Includes folded pedigree, 18-20th c., of Gloucestershire, Sussex, *etc.*

Dallingridge
SAUL, NIGEL. 'The rise of the Dallingridge family', *Sx.A.C.* **136**, 1998, 123-32. Medieval.
LOWER, MARK ANTONY. 'Notices of Sir Edward Dalyngruge, the builder of Bodiam Castle', *Sx.A.C.* **10**, 1860, 221-31. 14-15th c., includes genealogical notes.

Dalton
BASTIAN, F. 'The Dalton family of Leatherhead', *P.L.D.L.H.S.* **2**(9), 1965, 260-5. Includes pedigree, 16-19th c.

David
CHRISTOPHERS, R.A. 'The great Rees David mystery', *Sy.A.C.* **64**, 1967, 168-70. Discussions of various 16th c. clergymen of this name.

Davies
CHAPMAN, JULIANNE. 'Hot gossip', *E.Sy.F.H.S.J.* **17**(1), 1994, 25-7. Davies, Colbourn, and Brownings of Camberwell, *etc.*, 19th c.

Dawes
DALLEY, EMMA. 'The Dawes connection: Putney and the Dawes family', *Wandsworth historian* **47**, 1985, 25-7; **48**, 1986, 21-7. 16-17th c.
See also Willoughby

Day
JOHN, JUNE. 'Found in a copy of *Pilgrims Progress* and other works with notes', *F.R.* **5**(2), 1990, 31. Lists births and marriages of the Day family, 1813-1903.

De La Warr
STEVENS F. BENTHAM. 'The De La Warr family', *Sx.N.Q.* **17**, 1968-71, 26-8. 17-19th c.

De Mara
MALDEN, HENRY ELLIOT. 'Ashted and the De Mara chantry', *Sy.A.C.* **19**, 1906, 27-32. Includes pedigree shewing connection of De Mara, De Montfort, Freville and Boteler, 13-14th c.

De Montfort
See De Mara

Dearling
SPENCER, BILL. 'Oh my Dearlings!' *E.Sy.F.H.S.J.* **22**(4), 1991, 31-4. Dearling family of South London, 19th c.

Della Rocca
GREEN, CHRIS. 'The Della Rocca family', *E.Sy.F.H.S.J.* **16**(1), 1993, 9-15. Of Lambeth, *etc.*, 18-20th c.

Delves
See Humphrey

Dendy

COLLINS, WILLIAM J., SIR. 'Some memorials of the Dendy family', *Transactions of the Baptist Historical Society* **5**(3), 1917, 129-43. Of Sussex and Surrey, 16-18th c.

Dene

SALZMANN, L.F. 'Some Sussex Domesday tenants, II. The family of Dene', *Sx.A.C.* **58**, 1916, 171-88. Includes pedigree, 11-14th c., shewing descent via Icklesham to Heringaud.

Denham

HEHIR, BRENDAN O. 'The family of Denham of Egham, *Sy.A.C.* **64**, 1967, 71-85. 16-17th c.
See also Bond

Denison

BODDINGTON, REGINALD STEWART. 'Pedigree of the family of Denison, *M.G.H.* 2nd series **1**, 1886, 148. See also 180 & 248. Of Yorkshire and Surrey, 18-19th c.

Denyer

DENYER, RON. *The Denyers of Surrey and their genealogies.* 2 pts. Middleton: Ron Denyer, 1993.
DENYER, RON. *The Denyers of Sussex and their genealogies.* Middleton: Ron Denyer, 1991-2.

Devenish

DEVENISH, BERTHA, ed. *Archives of the Devenish family collected by Henry Weston Devenish.* Weymouth: J.H.C. & B. Devenish, 1933. Of Hampshire, Sussex and Dorset.
DEVENISH, ROBERT, & MCLAUGHLIN, N. CHARLES. *Historical and genealogical records of the Devenish families of England and Ireland ...* Chicago: Lakeside Press, 1948. Of Dorset and Sussex.

Dibble

BOWERMAN, LES. 'The Dibble family at the Anchor in Ripley', *Send & Ripley History Society newsletter* **131**, 1996, 7-10. 19-20th c.

Dicker

DICKER, GEOFFREY. *The family face.* Edinburgh: Pentland Press, 1998. Dicker family. Includes pedigrees, 18-20th c.

Digby

'Digby family', *Wandsworth notes and queries* **6**, 1899, 116-7. Early 18th c.

Digges

'Digges of Reigate', *Sy.A.C.* **1**, 1858, 239. Pedigree, medieval-17th c.

Dilloway

J[ERROME], P.A. 'Documents concerning the Dilloway family', *Petworth Society bulletin* **25**, 1981, 15-16. 19th c.

Dixon

HAYWARD, G. 'The Dixon family of Cherkley Court, Leatherhead', *P.L.D.L.H.S.* 3(9), 1975, 316-20; 3(10), 1976, 351-7; 4(3), 1979, 73-82. 19-20th c.

Dobell

BLAAUW, W.H. 'On Streat Place, the ancient manor of the Dobells', *Sx.A.C.* **4**, 1851, 93-100. Notes on the family, 17-18th c., with brief extracts from Williams Dobell's account book, 1708-42.
RADCLIFFE, ALAN FENWICK. 'Dobell of Streat', *Sx.A.C.* **66**, 1925, 123-35. 16-18th c.; includes folded pedigree of Lane, 17-19th c.

Dodson

ELLIS, WILLIAM SMITH. 'On the origin of the family of Dodson of Hurstpierpoint', *Sx.A.C.* **33**, 1883, 39-48. Includes folded pedigree, 17-19th c., also of Dodson of Cornwall, 15-17th c.

Domesday

EXCELL, STANLEY. 'Domesday in Horsham', *Sx.F.H.* 7(2), 1986, 43-5. Domesday family; includes pedigree, 16-17th c.

Dorling

DORLING, E.E. *Epsom and the Dorlings.* Stanley Paul & Co., 1939. 18-19th c.

Dormer
'Descent of Elizabeth, daughter and heir of Edward Dormer, esq., of Fulham, wife of John Gresham of Mayfield, Sussex, 1578', *M.G.H.* N.S. **4,** 1884, 97-9. Medieval.

Douglas
BARKER, D.J. 'The house of Douglas: a Bookham nursery', *P.L.D.L.H.S.* **5**(9), 1996, 234-8. 19-20th c.

Drake
BLACKMAN, MICHAEL E. 'The Drake family of Esher and Walton-on-Thames', *Sy.A.C.* **76,** 1985, 89-99. 16-18th c.
DRAKE, WILLIAM R., SIR. 'Some account of Richard Drake, of Esher Place, *temp.* Queen Elizabeth', *Sy.A.C.* **7,** 1880, 203-13. Includes brief pedigree of the Drake family of Reigate, 17th c.
'Relationship of Richard Drake of Esher, Co.Surrey, and Sir Francis Drake, kt., of Buckland Monachorum, Admiral', *Sy.A.C.* **52,** 1952, 88. 16th c.

Drew
ELLACOTT, PETER, 'Martha Drew of Densworth in Funtington: her husbands and their families', *Sx.F.H.* **13**(3), 1998, 73-81. 17th c. Drew connections with Bradshaw, Gunter, Norton and Gordon families.

Du Moulin-Browne
C., I.M. 'Du Moulin-Browne of Easebourne, and Moore of Fawley', *Genealogist* N.S. **8,** 1892, 30-33. 18-19th c.

Duke
BULTITUDE, HELEN. 'My ancestors were Dukes', *H. & R.F.H.S.J.* **10**(4), 1995, 70-71. 19th c.

Duly
See Baldy

Duncomb(e)
HALL, D.W., & HOMER, R.F. 'The Duncombes displayed', *The journal of the Pewter Society* 3(1), 1981, 19. Includes pedigree of Duncombe of Albury and Bewdley, Worcestershire, 17-18th c.

HOMER, RONALD F., & HALL, DAVID W. 'The Duncumbs, pewterers of Wribbenhall', *Journal of the Pewter Society* **4**(4), 1984, 128-32. Includes pedigree, 17-18th c. Of Surrey, Bewdley, *etc.*

Dunstanville
BENSON, J. 'The de Dunstanville's', *Devon and Cornwall notes and queries* **20,** 1938-9, 194-204. Of Shropshire, Sussex, Wiltshire, Devon and Cornwall; medieval, including pedigree.

Dupuis
BULLOCK-WEBSTER, A. 'The Dupuis family', *Proceedings of the Huguenot Society of London* **2,** 1887-8, 162-5. Of London, Surrey and Oxfordshire, *etc.*

Dutry
'Dutry', *M.G.H.* 2nd series **1,** 1886, 225. See also 234. Includes pedigree, 17-18th c.

Dyer
DYER, DAVE. 'William Dyer: blood and thunder preacher', *F.R.* **4**(3), 1990, 59-61. 17th c.
MUNCEY, FRANCES. 'A South Street tailor's business and family', *E.L.H.* **107,** 1998, 8-11. Dyer family of Eastbourne, 18-19th c.

Dysart
See Tollemache

Eatwell
See Harbroe

Edes
STEER, FRANCIS W. *The John Edes House, West Street, Chichester.* Chichester papers **52.** Chichester: Chichester City Council, 1968. Includes folded pedigree of Edes, 17-19th c.

Egles
'The Egles family of East Sussex', *Sx.G.L.H.* 3(2), 1981, 63-7. 16-19th c.

Eldridge
WILSON, E. 'Eldridge & Cruttenden', *H. & R.F.H.S.J.* **10**(2), 1995, 30-33. 19-20th c.

Eliot

C., H. 'Note to Manning and Bray's *History of Surrey,* vol.I, page 618: pedigree of Eliot of Godalming', *Sy.A.C.* **15**, 1900, 159. 16th c.

Elliot

See Spooner

Ellis

'Sussex pedigrees: Ellis of Burwash', *M.G.H.* 5th series **10**, 1938, 103. 18-19th c.

Elphick

ELPHICK, GEORGE. 'The history of a name', *D.P.H.S.M.* **3**(9), 1989, 23-30. Elphick family surname origins, *etc.*

Engleheart

BOLTON, IRIS PEROWNE. 'A Kew family of artists: a brief survey of the Engleheart and Richmond families', *R.H.* **12**, 1991, 53-7. Includes pedigree, 18-19th c.

Etchingham

HALL, SPENCER. *Echyngham of Echyngham.* George Barclay, 1850.

SAUL, NIGEL. *Scenes from provincial life: knightly families in Sussex, 1280-1400.* Oxford: Clarendon Press, 1986. Study of three Sussex families, i.e. Etchingham, Sackville, and Waleys.

MARTIN, DAVID. 'Three moated sites in North-East Sussex. Part 1. Glottenham', *Sx.A.C.* **127**, 1989, 89-122. Includes note on 'Glottenham and the Etchingham family', by Nigel Saul. Medieval.

SAUL, NIGEL. 'Some Etchingham ephemera, or, more scenes from provincial life', *Sx.A.C.* **127**, 1989, 254-5. Etchingham family, medieval. Brief note.

Etherington

'Etherington family bible', *Sx.F.H.* **8**(7), 1989, 322. 19th c.

Ettridge

See Collins

Eu, Earls of

ELLIS, WILLIAM SMITH. 'Observations on the Earls of Eu, and some of their presumed descendants', *Sx.A.C.* **10**, 1858, 63-8. Includes pedigrees, 10-13th c.

Evelyn

ELMSLIE, JAMES. 'The search for John Evelyn', *R. & B.* **14**(3), 1987, 84-6. Houghton and Evelyn families, 18-19th c.

EVELYN, HELEN. *The history of the Evelyn family.* Evelyn Nash, 1915. Of Wotton and Godstone, Wiltshire, *etc.* includes pedigrees, medieval-20th c.

FOLJAMBE, CECIL G.S. *Evelyn pedigrees and memoranda.* Privately printed, 1893. Not seen.

FOLJAMBE, CECIL G.S. 'Evelyn of Wotton and Sayes Court, and Evelyn of Woodcote', *M.G.H.* 2nd series **5**, 1894, 209-11. Pedigree, 17-18th c.

FOLJAMBE, CECIL G.S. 'The last male descendants of John Evelyn of Wotton, author of the 'diary', on the extinction of which line the Baronetcy became extinct', *M.G.H.* 2nd series **5**, 1894, 225-7. 17-19th c.

FOLJAMBE, CECIL G.S. 'Pedigree of George Raymond Evelyn, father of the twelfth Earl of Rothes (of Leslie, Co.Fife, and of Shrub Hill, near Dorking, Surrey)', *M.G.H.* 2nd series **5**, 1894, 177-9. 17-19th c.

FOLJAMBE, CECIL G.S. 'Pedigree of the Evelyns of Ireland, since of Wotton, Co.Surrey, Sayes Court, Deptford, and St.Clere, Kent', *M.G.H.* 2nd series **5**, 1894, 145-7. 17-19th c.

FOLJAMBE, CECIL G.S. 'Skeleton pedigree of the Evelyn family in all its branches', *M.G.H.* 2nd series **4**, 1892, 121-5. 15-19th c.

HISCOCK, W.G. *John Evelyn and his family circle.* Routledge & Kegan Paul, 1955. Includes brief pedigree, 17-18th c.

'Evelyn of Godstone, afterwards of America', *M.G.H.* 2nd series **5**, 1894, 201. Pedigree, 17-18th c.

'Evelyn of Godstone, Co.Surrey', *M.G.H.* 2nd series **4**, 1892, 337-42. 17-19th c.

'Evelyn of Kingston, Godstone, West Dean, Everley, etc', *M.G.H.* 2nd series **4**, 1892, 329. Pedigree, 17th c.

'Evelyn of Long Ditton, Co.Surrey', *M.G.H.* 2nd series **4**, 1892, 312-4. 17-19th c.

'Family of Evelyn of Wotton, Co.Surrey', *M.G.H.* 2nd series **5**, 1894, 202-3. Pedigree, 17-18th c.

'Genealogical memoronda relating to the family of Evelyn', *M.G.H.* 2nd series **1**, 1886, 1-2, 82-3, 100, 152-6, 176-7, 210, 222-3, 229-34, 258-9, 296-7, 319-22, 332 & 352-6; **2**, 1888, 8-11, 24-5, 38-9, 135-8, 184-6, 229, 245, 312 & 327-8; **3**, 1890, 242-5, 267-8, 269-71 & 298-300. Of Surrey, Wiltshire and Hampshire; includes pedigrees, 16-18th c.; monumental inscriptions, parish register extracts, marriage licences, *etc.*

Everington

'Entries re. Everington family in old Bible', *Hampshire family historian* **15**(4), 1989, 236-7. Of Herne Hill and South Dulwich, 19th c.

Evershed

EVERSHED, P.B. 'A cautionary tale', *Sx.F.H.* **8**(5), 1989, 232-3. Evershed family, 16-17th c.

EVERSHED, J.D. 'An extended family search', *Sx.F.H.* **7**(1), 1986, 27-31. Evershed family study.

EVERSHED, P.B. 'The family of fifteen, or, how to get a lot out of the G.R.O. index', *Sx.F.H.* **7**(7), 1987, 272-3. Evershed family, 19-20th c.

EVERSHED, P.B. 'Linked at last', *Sx.F.H.* **12**(4), 1996, 125-6. Evershed family, 16-18th c.
See also Mitchell and Young

Eversfield

ISHAM, GYLES, SIR, & TOYNBEE, MARGARET. 'Sir Thomas Eversfield, M.P. for Hastings and his two wives, Elizabeth (Goring) and Jane (Alford)', *Sx.N.Q.* **14**, 1954-7, 253-62. 16-17th c.

'The Eversfields', *Hindsight: the journal of the Uckfield & District Preservation Society* **1**, 1995, 34-5. Includes pedigrees, 16-17th c.

Fairall

JAQUES, JULIETTE. 'Fairalls of Godstone', *L.H.R.* **29**, 1990, 37-40. 20th c.

JAQUES, JULIETTE W. 'The Fairalls of Godstone and Caterham', *E.Sy.F.H.S.* **13**(1), 1990, 21-6. 19th c.

Farmer

TURNER, STEPHEN. 'Three generations make a gentleman: the story of the Farmer family of Nonsuch Park', *Surrey history* **1**(5), 1977/8, 203-12. Includes pedigree, 18-20th c.

Farrer

FARRER, THOMAS CECIL, LORD. *Some Farrer memorials, being a selection from the papers of Thomas Henry, first Lord Farrer, 1819-1899, on various matters connected with his life, with notes relating to some branches of the family of Greystoneley, Ingleborough, Abinger, between 1610 and 1923.* G. Sherwood, 1923. Includes pedigrees. 17-20th c.

Fauntleroy

'The genealogy of Robert Fauntleroy, of the Borough of Southwark, in the County of Surrey, merchant, third son of Robert Fauntleroy of Culvers Grove, in the parish of Boreham, in the county of Essex, shewing his descent from the ancient family of Fauntleroy of Fauntleroys Marsh, in the County of Dorset', *Fragmenta genealogica* **7**, 1902, 44-5. 16-18th c.

Fenn

FENN, G.E. 'A marriage settlement', *R. & B.* **24**(4), 1998, 154-5. Fenn family, 18th c.

Fenner

LONGHURST, T.J. ed. *Fenner family records.* [ ]: International Research Publications, 1975. Medieval-19th c.; of Kent, Sussex and many other counties.

Fetherstonhaugh

MEADE-FETHERSTONHAUGH, MARGARET, & WARNER, OLIVER. *Uppark and its people.* George Allen & Unwin, 1964. Descent, especially in the Fetherstonhaugh family, 18-20th c.

Field

FIELD, GRAHAM. 'William and Elizabeth Field of Brighton', *Sx.F.H.* **7**(7), 1987, 284-5.

Fielder

DORRINGTON, J.B., & FIELDER, C. *Fielder family records.* International Research Publications, 1975. Of Sussex, Surrey, Hampshire, Kent, *etc.* Includes many extracts from parish registers and other sources, 16-19th c.

Finch

FINCH, JOYCE, & FINCH, JOHN. *Jane Finch and her family.* Worthing: Denham House, 1974. Of Buckinghamshire and Surrey; includes folded pedigree, 18-20th c.

PHILIPOTT, JO. 'Finch genealogy', *M.G.H.* **2**, 1876, 325-37. Of Kent and Sussex, *etc.,* medieval.

ROUND, J. HORCAE. 'The origin of the Finches', *Sx.A.C.* **70**, 1929, 19-31. Medieval.

Fisher
See Willoughby

Fitzalan

HALL, HAMILTON. 'The Fitzalan pedigree', *Sx.A.C.* **37**, 1890, 183-5. Medieval.

Fitzgilbert

TURNER, DENNIS. 'The Norman owners of Blechingley Castle: a review', *Sy.A.C.* **83**, 1996, 37-56. Includes pedigree of the ancestors of Richard Fitzgilbert, 10-11th c.

Florance

FLORANCE, SANDRA. 'Florances of England and Australia', *Sx.F.H.* **14**(1), 2000, 12-13. 18-19th c.

Fogden

REYNOLDS, JOHN. 'My Donnington ancestors in the 18th & 19th centuries', *Sx.F.H.* **11**(8), 1995, 279-83. Fogden, Prior and Reynolds families; includes pedigree, 18-20th c.

Folkes

PERRY, N.R. 'A Surrey ancestry: Folkes/Fookes/Fulk', *R. & B.* **1**(3), 1975, 103-6. 18-19th c.

Fookes
See Folkes

Forbes

BELLEW, GEORGE. 'Who was this Edward Forbes?' *F.M.S.Q.N.* **8**(9), 1989, 165-74. Includes notes on Forbes family, 18th c.

Fortescue
See Locke King

Frederick

'Frederick', *M.G.H.* 3rd series **2**, 1898, 134. Of London and Walton on Thames, Surrey; extract from family bible, 18th c.

Freeman

FREEMAN, R.F. 'The Freeman search: London and Sussex', *Sx.F.H.* **9**(7), 1991, 243-52. See also **10**(2), 1992, 72-3. Includes pedigree, 17-20th c.

Freville
See De Mars

Frewen

CHAMBERLAIN, JEFFREY S. 'Portrait of a High Church clerical dynasty in Georgian England: the Frewens and their world', in WALSH, JOHN, HAYDON, COLIN, & TAYLOR, STEPHEN, eds. *The Church of England, c. 1689-c.1833: from Toleration to Tractarianism.* Cambridge: Cambridge Universty Press, 1993, 299-316. *See also* Blaxton

Fulham

BRAY, W. 'Pedigree of the family of Fulham, of Compton, Surrey', *Collectanea topographica et genealogica* **1**, 1834, 17-19. 17-18th c.

Fulk

PERRY, NIGEL. 'The Fulk family of West Horsley, Surrey', *R. & B.* **4**(2), 1977, 49-52; **4**(3), 1978, 82-6. Medieval-18th c. *See also* Folkes

Fuller

BLACKMAN, HERBERT. 'Gun founding at Heathfield in the XVIII century', *Sx.A.C.* **67**, 1926, 25-54. Transcripts of original sources relating to the business of the Fuller family.

DOFF, ELIZABETH. 'The Robertson memorial lecture: the Fullers of Brightling Park', *Battle and District Historical Society newsletter* **5**, 1987, 14-16. 18th c.

FULLER, J.F. 'Pedigree of the family of Fuller of Waldron and East Hoathley, *etc',* *M.G.H.* 4th series **3**, 1910, 166-73. 16-19th c.

PARKS, ALEC. *The Fuller's progress: a study of a remarkable Sussex family, 16-19th centuries.* [Heathfield]: Heathfield and Waldron Community Association, 1988.

SALT, MARY C.L. 'The Fullers of Brightling Park', *Sx.A.C.* **104,** 1966, 63-87; **106,** 1968, 73-88; **107,** 1969, 14-24. 16-18th c.

THOMPSETT, MICHAEL. 'The Fuller family of Brighton', *Sx.F.H.* **13**(7), 1999, 241-2. 19th c.

SAVILLE, R.V. 'Gentry wealth on the Weald in the eighteenth century: the Fullers of Brightling Park', *Sx.A.C.* **121,** 1983, 129-47.

THOMAS, J.R. 'Who was Great-great-great-granny Fuller? Proving her identity', *Sx.F.H.* **10**(6), 1993, 225-7. 19th c.

'Fuller of London, Tandridge Court, etc.', *M.G.H.* 5th series **1,** 1916, 253-9. Pedigree, 17-19th c.

See also Nutt

Funnell
'Funnell', *D.P.H.S.M.* **2**(7), 1984, 13-14. 19th c.

Furmage
FRIEND, BERYL. *Named after my ancestors: a family history.* [Uckfield]: the author, 1984. Furmage family; includes folded pedigree, 18-20th c.

Gage
STEINMAN, G. STEINMAN. *Some account of the manor of Haling in the parish of Croydon, Surrey, with notices of the family of Gage of that place.* [ ], 1835. Partly reprinted from *Collectanea topographica et genealogica.* 15-19th c., includes pedigrees of Gardyner, Parker and Hamond.

Gainsford
GAINSFORD, WILLIAM DUNN, ed. *Annals of the house of Gainsford, sometime of the counties of Surrey, Oxon., Monmouth, Nottingham, Lincoln & Kent, between the years A.D. 1331 and A.D. 1909.* Horncastle: W.K.Morton & Sons, 1909. Includes pedigrees and many extracts from original sources. Supplemented by: CANTIANUS. 'The Gainsford of Carshalton', *Sy.A.C.* **27,** 1914, 143-4.

Gale
BLENCOWE, ROBERT WILLIS. 'Extracts from the memoirs of the Gale family', *Sx.A.C.* **12,** 1860. 45-60. See also **13,** 1861, 307-8. 17-18th c.

Gardiner
BASTIAN, F. 'Leatherhead families of the 16th and 17th centuries, V: Gardiner of Thorncroft', *P.L.D.L.H.S.* **2**(5), 1961, 135-44. Includes pedigree.

Gardyner
See Gage

Garland
RISNESS, ERIC. 'The Garland family at Petworth', *Petworth Society magazine* **63,** 1991, 15-17. 19th c.

Gass
See Guest

Gasson
'Gasson', *D.P.H.S.M.* **2**(7), 1984, 15-17. 17-19th c.

Gauder
MALDEN, H.E. 'Bondmen in Surrey under the Tudors', *Transactions of the Royal Historical Society* N.S., **19,** 1905, 305-7. Manumissions of the Gauder family, c.1581.

Gearing
GEARING, ALBERT. 'A long-lived family', *Sx.F.H.* **10**(2), 1992, 68-70. Gearing family of Patcham, Greenwich, *etc.,* 15-20th c.

Geering
GEERING, SHIRLEY. 'Can you help me? my cousin asked', *Sx.G.L.H.* **1**(1), 1979, 21-3. Geering family, 19th c.

George
HAYWARD, NINA. 'Did he walk or was he carried?', *R. & B.* **18**(3), 1991, 100-102. George family of Lambeth, 19th c.

Gerard
See Godman

Gervase
MCCANN, TIMOTHY J. 'Some notes on the family of George Gervase of Bosham, martyr', *Sx.A.C.* **113,** 1975, 152-6. 16-17th c.

Gess
GESS, T.J. 'Guess where?' *Sx.F.H.* **8**(8), 1989, 364-5. Gess/Guest/Gass family; includes pedigree, 19-20th c.

Gibb
TOLL, KEN. 'Gibb/Tester family bible', *Sx.F.H.* **10**(1), 1992, 20. Of Cuckfield and Uckfield, 19th c.

Gibbon(s)

GIBBONS, A.W. *Gibbons family notes: a collection of memoranda relating to the Gibwen, Gubion, Guibon and various branches of the Gibbon and Gibbons families.* Army and Navy Co-operative Society, 1884. Of many counties, but especially Lincolnshire, Kent, Sussex and Staffordshire, medieval-18th c. Includes many extracts from parish registers, notes on wills, *etc.*

Gibson

JEFFREE, RICHARD. 'The Gibson family of artists', *R.H.* **10,** 1989, 17-28. 17-18th c.

Gilbert

GILBERT, RICHARD. 'A Sussex evangelist', *Sx.N.Q.* **17,** 1968-71, 54-6. Family of George Gilbert of Rotherfield, 17-19th c.

Gillam

GILLAM, CLIFFORD W. 'The Gillams of Bolney & Brighton', *Sx.F.H.* **4**(8), 1981, 255-8. 18-19th c.
See also Collins

Gil(l)man

GILLMAN, ALEXANDER WILLIAM. *Searches into the history of the Gillman or Gilman family, including the various branches of England, Ireland, America and Belgium.* Elliot Stock, 1895. Includes folded pedigrees, medieval-19th c., with a chapter on the family in Surrey.

Gladwyshe

GLADWISH, VICTOR E.R. *The Rape of Hastings family of de Gladwyshe, 1225-1980.* Somersham: the author, 1981. Of Kent and Sussex; includes pedigrees.

Glue

CLARKE, DENNIS. 'The 18th century Glues of Harting', *Sx.F.H.* **13**(3), 1998, 98-9.

Glyn

ABDY, CHARLES. *The Glyns of Ewell: the story of a family from 1736 to 1946.* Ewell: the author, 1994.

Godman

BASTIAN, F. 'Leatherhead families of the 16th and 17th centuries, II. Godman, Gerard and Dacres', *P.L.D.L.H.S.* **2**(2), 1958, 43-52. See also **2**(5), 1961, 144; **2**(6), 1962, 186. Includes pedigree.

GODMAN, C. EDITH. *The thirteen children of Joseph and Caroline Godman of Park Hatch and their descendants: a genealogy, with tabular pedigrees.* Edgware: James V. Coate. 1971. 19-20th c.

GODMAN, PERCY S. *Some account of the family of Godman, with a record of every known reference to the name.* Privately printed, 1897. Mainly of Surrey and Sussex; also of Bristol, *etc.* Includes folded pedigrees.

Goffe

ARNOLD, HENRY E. B. 'A Sussex family during the Commonwealth', *Sussex county magazine* **10,** 1936, 668-72 & 740-43. Goffe family of Bramber cum Botolphs.

Gordon

See Drew

Gore-Brown

See Locke King

Goring

ARNOLD, H.E.B. 'The Gorings of Danny in the Civil War', *Sussex county magazine* **13,** 1939, 735-9.
See also Eversfield

Gorringe

HODSOLL, VERA. 'Farming families in Eastbourne', *E.L.H.S.N.* **41,** 1981, 3-5. Notes on the Gorringe family, 17-20th c.

Gott

HADDAN, ISABEL. 'The Sussex Gotts: the true history of Peter Gott, esq., knight of the shire, and Martha his wife (1650-1712)', *Sussex county magazine* **4,** 1930, 381-5.

Gounter

ARNOLD, F.H. 'Notes on the family of Gounter', *Sx.A.C.* **28,** 1878, 200-202. Medieval-17th c.

Gouyquet
WAGNER, HERBERT. 'Huguenot family of Gouyquet de St. Eloy', *M.G.H.* 4th series **1**, 1966, 70-71. Of Merton; pedigree, 18th c.

Grace
FLETCHER, J.S. 'Winchester and the Thames: what they have in common', *Hampshire family historian* **20**(1), 1993, 12-15; **20**(2), 1993, 121-5. Grace of Winchester; Mallett of Lambeth, Surrey. Includes pedigrees, 18-19th c.

Graham
GRAHAM, PAT. 'The Graham family: from Cumberland to Brighton and beyond', *Sx.F.H.* **12**(2), 1996, 55-6. 19th c.

Grantham
'Grantham family', *Sx.F.H.* **3**(6), 1978, 183-5. Of Lewes, *etc.,* 15-19th c.

Grantley
See Carrill

Gratwick(e)
COMBER, J. 'The family of Gratwicke, of Jarvis, Shermanbury, and Tortington', *Sx.A.C.* **60**, 1919, 34-66. Includes folded pedigrees, 16-18th c.; also, notes on the 'descent of Gratwicke estates', i.e. the manors of Seaford, Balsden, Itford, Ham, and Tortington.
'Pedigree of the family of Gratwick', *Reliquary* **18**, 1877-8, 220(f). Of Sussex, 16-17th c.

Green
GREEN, CHARLES ALFRED HOWELL. *Francis Green of Denmark Hill, Surrey, and his descendants.* 2nd ed. Devizes: George Simpson and Co., 1928. 18-20th c., also of various other counties.

Gresham
LEVESON GOWER, GRANVILLE. *Genealogy of the family of Gresham.* Mitchell and Hughes, 1883. Of London, Titsey, Mayfield, Holt in Norfolk, *etc.* Includes extensive pedigrees, medieval-19th c., and many extracts from original sources.

LEVESON GOWER, GRANVILLE. 'Gresham: genealogical memoranda relating to the family of Gresham', *M.G.H.* N.S. **1**, 1874, 373-5, 401-7 & 429-36. Extracts from the parish registers of Titsey and Limpsfield, and many other parishes in Surrey, Kent, Rutland, Suffolk, London, Norfolk, Gloucestershire, *etc.;* also dispensations, marriage allegations, monumental inscriptions, *etc.*
LEVESON-GOWER, R.H.G. 'The Greshams of Titsey', *E.Sy.F.H.S.J.* **2**(3), 1979, 14-18. Includes pedigree, 15-20th c.
'Pedigree of Gresham: pedigree B: Gresham of Titsey', *M.G.H.* N.S. **4**, 1884, 269-72 & 281-6. 16-17th c.
'Pedigree of Gresham of Holt, Co.Norfolk, and of Titsey and Limpsfield, Co.Surrey', *M.G.H.* N.S., **4**, 1884, 251-6. 14-16th c.
See also Dormer

Griffiths
GRIFFITHS, BERNARD. *In search of my ancestors.* Alresford: the author, 1995. Griffiths, Stockman, Tellick and Smith families of Cornwall, Devon, Hampshire, Surrey and Sussex; includes folded pedigees, 18-20th c.

Grover
ELLIS, W. SMITH. 'Some notes on the Grover family', *Sx.A.C.* **37**, 1890, 133-8. 16-19th c.

Grumbridge
COOK, ROBERT, & BURGESS, KENNETH M. 'Grumbridge: the spread of a surname', *E.Sy.F.H.S.J.* **3**(2), 1980, 11-13. In Surrey and Kent, *etc.,* 19-20th c.

Guest
See Gess

Guibon
See Gibbon(s)

Gunter
GUNTER, G.W., & VINER, G.A. 'Gunter in Wales and Sussex', *W.Sx.H.* **32**, 1985, 1-6; **33**, 1986, 14-22. Includes pedigrees, medieval-18th c.
See also Drew

Hack

GOLDEN, JACQUELINE. 'From Sussex to Australia: the emigration of the Hack family', *W.Sx.H.* **18**, 1981, 3-5.

Hackblock

GOLLIN, G.J. 'John Hackblock and his Copthorne estate', *P.L.D.L.H.S.* 4(6), 1982, 158-63. Includes pedigree, 19th c.

Haines

HAINES, CHARLES REGINALD. *A complete memoir of Richard Haines (1633-1685), a forgotten Sussex worthy, with a full account of his ancestry and posterity (continuing also chapters on the origin of the names Hayne and Haynes, and the various coats of arms associated with them.)* Harrison & Sons, 1899.

Hall

MARSHALL, GEORGE W. 'Family of Hall: additions to the visitation of London ... no. III', *M.G.H.* N.S. **1**, 1874, 127-31 & 457-76. Includes pedigrees of Hall of Horsham and London, 16-17th c; also of Ravenscroft of Horsham, 16-17th c.

Ham(m)ond

MILLER, RICHARD. 'The Hamond or Hammond family of Battle', *Sx.F.H.* 13(1), 1998, 26-7. 13-19th c.
See also Cooper and Gaye

Hampton

E., W.S. 'Pedigree of Hampton of Surrey and Sussex', *Collectanea topographica et genealogica* **6**, 1840, 294.

Harbottle

HOLLAND, MICHAEL. 'Harbottle - Holland families', *Sx.N.Q.* **2**, 1929, 244-5. 15-16th c.

Harbroe

SLATFORD, JOHN. 'Elm Tree House & Homewood Farm: 19c family connections in Ripley', *R. & B.* 19(4), 1993, 144-5. Harbroe and Eatwell families; includes pedigree.
SLATFORD, JOHN. 'Some 19th century family connections with Elm Tree House and Homewood Farm, both in Ripley, Surrey', *Send & Ripley History Society newsletter* **107**, 1992, 9-11. Includes pedigree of Harbroe and Eatwell, 19th c.

Harding

STONER, ALAN. 'The death and funeral of the father of an extraordinary family', *Sx.F.H.* 6(8), 1985, 285-6. Harding of Shipley, 19th c.

Hare

STEVENS, F. BENTHAM. 'Note on the Hares of Herstmonceux', *Sx.N.Q.* **13**, 1950-53, 157-8. 19th c.

Harman/Harmer

HARMAN, DAVID L.N. 'Harman or should they be Harmer?' *Sx.F.H.* 11(4), 1994, 139-40.
PRICE, GILL. 'Jonathan Harmer: stonemason & potter of Heathfield', *F.R.* 9(4), 1995, 79-81. 18th c., brief notes on the Harmer family.
Harmer family newsletter. [ ]: Harmer Family Association, 1978- . Last issue seen 8(4), 1985.
Harmers of Sussex. 2 vols. Chester: Harmer Family Association, 1990. v.1. Heathfield roots. v.2. Salehurst roots. Pedigrees, 16-20th c.

Hart

FERGUSON, PETER. 'The two Uckfield Richard Harts', *Hindsight: journal of the Uckfield & District Preservation Society* **2**, 1996, 14-16. Includes pedigree of Hart, 18-19th c.

Harvard

REDLE, W. 'Harvard University and the Harvards of Sussex', *Genealogist* N.S. **1**, 1884, 107-11. See also 182-3; **3**, 1886, 188.

Harvey

HARVEY, WILLIAM I. *Genealogy of the family of Harvey of Folkestone, Co.Kent, London, Hackney and Twickenham, Co.Middlesex, Croydon, Putney and Kingston, Co.Surrey; Hempstead, Chigwell and Barking, Co.Essex, Clifton and Wicke, Co.Dorset, etc.* Mitchell & Hughes, 1889. Pedigrees, 16-19th c. See also *M.G.H.* 2nd series **3**, 1890, 329-36, 362-5 & 381-4. Pedigree, 17-19th c.

Hastings

BEEVOR, R. J. *Hastings of Hastings.* Colchester: Ballantyne Press, 1931. Medieval-19th c.
See also Marchant

Hawarde

BAILDON, W. PALEY. *The Hawardes of Tandridge, Co.Surrey.* Spottiswoode & Co., 1894. Reprinted from the introduction to *Les reportes del cases in Camera Stellata,* by John Hawarde. 17th c.

Hawes

DOFF, ELIZABETH. 'The Hawes family of Salehurst, Berwick and Warbleton', *Sussex history* **21**, 1986, 20-23. Includes pedigrees, 16-18th c.

Hawkes

PARDOE, BERNARD. 'The note-book of Thomas Hawkes', *R. & B.* **10**(2), 1983, 54-6. Notes on the Hawkes family, 18-19th c.

Hawkins

'Hawkins: entries from a bible ...', *M.G.H.* 3rd series **3**, 1900, 8. Of Surrey; 18th c.
See also Boxall

Hayne(s)

See Haines

Hearsey

PEARSE, HUGH. *The Hearseys: five generations of an Anglo-Indian family.* Edinburgh: William Blackwood & Sons, 1905.

Heath

TICKNER, VINCENT. 'The Heaths: blacksmiths of Burpham and Stoke, 1755-1880', *R. & B.* **19**(4), 1993, 138-42.

Helps

POWELL, DOLORES E. *Queen Victoria's true and devoted friends.* Bristol: the author, 1977. Biography of Sir Arthur Helps of Balham; includes much genealogical information, with pedigree, 19th c.

Henty

BASSETT, MARNIE. *The Hentys: an Australian colonial tapestry.* Oxford University Press, 1954. Originally of Sussex.
MORRIS, MARJORIE. 'The Hentys: a Worthing family', *W.Sx.H.* **37**, 1987, 18-24. 19th c. emigrants to Portland, Australia.

Heringaud

See Dene

Heron

S[TEINMAN], G.S. 'Pedigree of Heron, of Addiscombe, Surrey', *Collectanea topographica et genealogica* **2**, 1835, 166-7.

Hewitt

HEWETT, REGINALD GUY. 'Tribute to four generations', *L.H.R.* **33**, 1994, 41-4. Hewett family of Caterham, 19-20th c.

Hidar, Hidder, Hider

See Hyder

Hilder

GOLLIN, G.J. 'The Hilder house in Farm Lane, Ashtead', *P.L.D.L.H.S.* **4**(7), 1983, 184-7. 17-18th c.

Hilton

'Who told the lie?' *Sx.F.H.* **13**(1), 1998, 17-19. Hilton family, 16-18th c.

Hoard

ELLIS, W.S. 'Hoard or Howard of Ewell and Guilford, Co.Surrey', *M.G.H.* N.S. **4**, 1884, 137-43, 267-8, 288-90 & 296-9. See also 273. Includes pedigrees, wills, parish register extracts, *etc.,* 17-19th c. Actually Guildford.

Hoare

HOARE, RICHARD COLT, SIR. *Pedigrees and memoirs of the families of Hore of Rishford, Com. Devon, Hoare of Walton, Com. Bucks, Hoare of London, Com. Middlesex., Hoare of Stourton, Com. Wilts., Hoare of Barn-Elms, Com. Surrey; Hoare of Boreham, Com. Essex.* Bath: Richard Cruthwell, 1819. Includes pedigrees, medieval-19th c.
See also Locke King

Hobbs

HOBBS, COLIN. 'The family of Hobbs in Fletching', *D.P.H.S.M.* **5**(8), 1996, 8-11. 18-19th c.

Hoffmester

AUBREY, T.B. 'Additional sources for a family history: the Hoffmeisters', *R. & B.* **3**(2), 1976, 74-7. 18-20th c.

Hofland
BELL, PHYLLIS. 'The Hoflands at Richmond', *R.H.* **2**, 1981, 3-7. 18-19th c.

Holden/Holder
LEESON, FRANK. 'Holden versus Holder', *Sx.F.H.* **11**(8), 1995, 286. Holden and Holder families, medieval.

Holkham
HOLKHAM, TONY. 'Is there anyone there?' *Sx.F.H.* **12**(5), 1997, 189-90. Holkham family of Aldwick, 19th c.

Holland
See Harbottle

Holmes
See Bax

Homewood
BIRD, RUTH. 'Homewood of Fletching', *Sx.G.L.H.* **1**(1), 1979, 27. 17-18th c.

Hone
HONE, JIM. 'The family of Hone', *Send & Ripley History Society newsletter* **91**, 1990, 4-6; **92**, 1990, 2.

Honeysett
HUNNISETT, R.F. 'Honeysett', *Sx.N.Q.* **16**, 1963-7, 172-4. Surname study, medieval; of Buckinghamshire and East Sussex. *etc.*

Honywood
ELLIS, WILLIAM SMITH. 'The pedigree of Honywood of Horsham', *Genealogist* N.S., **4**, 1887, 22-4. 16-17th c.

Hoo
See Braose

Hooker
ALLAN, MEA. *The Hookers of Kew, 1785-1911.* Michael Joseph, 1967. Includes folded pedigree 16-20th c., shewing connexion with Turner and Vincent.
HOOKER, RAY. 'Descent from the Kings: another cousin', *R. & B.* **5**(2), 1978, 44-7. Hooker family descent, 12-20th c.

Hord
E., W.S. 'Pedigree of the family of Hord, of Salop, Oxon., and Surrey', *Topographer and genealogist* **1**, 1846, 33-42.

Horde
See Roberts

Hore
See Hoare

Horne
CLARKE, BASIL E. 'Sussex pedigrees: Horne of Brede', *M.G.H.* 5th series **10**, 1938, 52-3. 17-19th c.
'The Sussex ancestors of an Anglian bishop: the Hornes of Brede', *Sx.G.L.H.* **2**(4), 1981, 164-6. 17-18th c.

Hoskins
See Master

Houghton
See Evelyn

Howard
BECKETT, ARTHUR. 'House of Howard', *Sussex county magazine* **3**, 1929, 296-312. See also 585. Medieval-20th c.
BRADBROOK, WILLIAM. 'Howard', *M.G.H.* 3rd series **4**, 1902, 191-5. Extracts from the parish registers of Cobham, Surrey and Bethnal Green, Middlesex, 17-19th c.
BRENAN, GERALD, & STATHAM, EDWARD PHILLIPS. *The house of Howard.* 2 vols. Hutchinson & Co., 1907.
BURCHALL, MICHAEL J. 'The deputy Earls Marshall and the Howard family', *Sx.G.L.H.* **5**(3), 1983, 91-4. 15-20th c.
GATTY, ALFRED. *The noble and illustrious family of Howard: a lecture delivered in Sheffield, in 1879.* Sheffield: Leader and Sons, 1899.
GOLLIN, G.J. & LEVER, R.A. 'The ownership of Ashtead manor', *P.L.D.L.H.S.* **4**(4), 1980, 110-12. In the Howard family; includes pedigree, 1688-1877.
LEVESON-GOWER, GRANVILLE. 'The Howards of Effingham', *Sy.A.C.* **9**, 1888, 395-436. Includes folded pedigree, 15-19th c., extracts from parish registers, monumental inscriptions, funeral certificates, wills, *etc.*

43

PAGET, FRANCES EDWARD. *Some records of the Ashtead estate, and of its Howard possessors, with notices of Elford, Castle Rising, Levens and Charlton.* Lichfield: Alfred Charles Lomax, 1873. 14-19th c.; includes extracts from registers at Elford, Ashtead, Saffron Walden, and Charlton.

ROBINSON, JOHN. *The Dukes of Norfolk.* Rev. ed. Chichester: Phillimore, 1995. Howard family, of Norfolk, Suffolk, Sussex, Derbyshire etc., 13-20th c.

See also Hoard

Hudson
BYFORD, ERIC C. 'The Hudson family of Hartfield', *Sx.F.H.* **12**(7), 1997, 247-8. Early 20th c.

RAYNER, OLIVE. 'Perseverance rewarded', *Family tree magazine* **15**(9), 1999, 48-9. Hudson family, 19th c.

Huffey
HUFFEY, GILLIAN. 'The Huffeys of Hastings', *Sx.F.H.* **4**(3), 1980, 86-8. 20th c.

Humphrey
CHITTY, ROSE. 'The Humphrey brothers: a story of the early days of cricket', *E.Sy.F.H.S.J.* **21**(3), 1998, 38-41. 19th c.

FITCETT, PAULINE. *My dear brother: a family history: Humphrey, Delves, Cleaver.* Wellington, N.Z: the author, 1989. Of Sussex and New Zealand; mainly 19-20th c.

Hunnisett
HUNNISETT, HEDLEY T. 'History and origin of the surname Hunnisett', *Sx.F.H.* **10**(4), 1992, 147-52. Of Sussex and Kent, includes list of births, marriages and deaths, 1517-1875 in both counties.

HUNNISETT, HENRY. 'One Hunnisett family', *Sx.F.H.* **5**(5), 1983, 150-59. Includes pedigree.

Hurdis
TIBBLE, RONALD. 'Rev. Thomas Hurdis, Ll.B. (1673-1733), *Sx.F.H.* **10**(3), 1992, 102-5. Of Ringmer.

Hyder
LUGARD, CECIL E. *Some notes of the family of Hyder (Hidar, Hidder, Hider, Hyedar, Hydare, Hyddor) of Sussex & Kent.* Rhyl: the author, 1942. 16-19th c.

Hyland
GLENN, T.A. *The family of Hyland, of Harmony Hall Plantation in the province of Maryland, and formerly of the counties of Kent and Sussex in old England.* Harrison and Sons, 1929. Includes pedigree, 16-19th c.

Icklesham
See Dene

Ide
MARSH, R. 'A cherry from Oving', *E.Sy.F.H.S.J.* **17**(3), 1994, 33-4. Ide family, 19-20th c.

MARSH, RONALD. 'The Ide family', *Sx.F.H.* **10**(1), 1992, 133-4. Included pedigrees, 18-20th c.

Isted
ISTED, BRUCE RAYMOND. 'Researching the Isted family', *F.R.* **3**(2), 1988, 6-8. Brief note, 16-20th c.

Jackman
GRENFELL, DIANA. 'The Jackmans and their plants: a history of the Woking nursery 1810-1972', *Surrey history* **3**(1), 1984/5, 29-40.

James
C., R.C. 'Family of James, of London, Essex, Kent, Suffolk and Surrey', *East Anglian* **1**, 1858-63, 330-31. 16-19th c.

PARRATT, JEAN. 'Keeping time with the James family', *F.M.S.Q.N.* **11**(8), 1997, 123-4. 19th c.

Jarritt
SCHOMBERG, ARTHUR. 'Jarritt', *M.G.H.* 3rd series **2**, 1898, 60. Of London and Parham.

Jarvis
ANGUS, CAROL. 'The moving family', *Sx.F.H.* **13**(5), 1999, 151-3. Jarvis family, 18-20th c.

Jeake
SMART, T.W.W. 'A biographical sketch of Samuel Jeake, senr., of Rye', *Sx.A.C.* **13**, 1861, 57-79. Includes pedigree, 16-18th c.

Jeffery

BARBER, GEOFFREY GLENN. 'Benjamin Jeffery & his letters', *Sx.F.H.* **8**(3), 1988, 86-91. Includes pedigree, 19-20th c.

Jekyll

PRATT, PATRICIA. 'The Jekyll family and Bramley House', *Bramley History Society newsletter* **12**, 1998, 12-17. See also **13**, 1998, 13-15. 19th c.

Jennings/Jenyas

'Jennings (Jenyns) of Surrey and Sandridge, Herts.', *M.G.H.* 5th series **8**, 1932-4, 89-90. Pedigree, 15-17th c.

Jordan

See Bullie

Jupp

KAY, JENNIFER. 'Farmer of this parish', *E.Sy.F.H.S.J.* **20**(2), 1997, 37-41; **20**(3), 1997, 34-9. Jupp family of Bindley Heath and Outwood, 19-20th c.

Kaye

PUCKLE, R.K. *Pedigree of the Wandsworth Common branch of the Kaye family.* Rev. ed. [ ], 1910. 18-19th c.

Kearton

KEARTON, CHERRY. 'The Keartons of Caterham', *L.H.R.* **6**, 1967, 15-20. 20th c.

Kelly

FERGUSON, PETER. 'Uckfield House: the Kelly connection', *Hindsight: the journal of the Uckfield & District Preservation Society* **3**, 1997, 11-18. Includes pedigree of Kelly, 18th c.

Kemp(e)

DALE, ANTONY. 'The Kemp family in Lewes and Brighton', *Sx.F.H.* **8**(3), 1988, 100-107. Includes pedigree, 18-19th c.

HITCHIN-KEMP, FRED. *A general history of the Kemp and Kempe families of Great Britain and her colonies ...* Leadenhall Press, 1902. Of Kent, Norfolk, Suffolk, Essex, Middlesex, Cornwall, Sussex, *etc.* Includes pedigrees, medieval-19th c.

Kempsall

FROST, A.J. 'Across the border: the Kempsall family', *Sx.F.H.* **8**(5), 1989, 209-10. 16-17th c.

Kesingland

See Poppy

Keynes

SALZMAN, L.F. 'Sussex domesday tenants, III. William de Cahagnes and the family of Keynes', *Sx.A.C.* **63**, 1922, 180-202. Includes folded pedigree, 11-14th c.

Kidd

See Bax

Kidder

TURNER, EDWARD. 'Richard Kidder, Bishop of Bath and Wells, and the Kidders of Maresfield', *Sx.A.C.* **9**, 1857, 125-38. Includes pedigrees, 15-19th c.

King

ALDRIDGE, C. PEGGY. 'Genealogy of the King family', *Send & Ripley History Society newsletter* **104**, 1992, 8-11. Includes pedigree, 18-20th c.

KING, ALBERT. 'The Kings of Kings Hill Cottage', *Sx.F.H.* **11**(8), 1995, 291-2. At Burwash, 19th c.

See also Locke King

Kipling

HOPKINS, R. THURSTON. 'The Kipling family', *Sussex county magazine* **4**, 1930, 547-53. 19th c.

Kirby

PIKE, ISABEL. 'The Kirby family of Mayfield', *Sx.G.L.H.* **2**(2), 1980, 75-9. 17-20th c.

Knight

BREMNER, ANN. 'A Knight in Merton: an account of the search for William Harold Knight (1867-1950) tapestry weaver and stained glass artist and designer with Morris & Co. (circa 1881-1940)', *Family history* **19**(157); N.S. **132**, 1998, 152-60. Includes pedigree, 19-20th c; this family was also of Islington, Middlesex. Also mentions Kidner family of Lambeth.

Tickner (King column top)

TICKNER, VINCENT. 'Seeking the origins of Edmund Kemp (1700?-1759) of Trotton', *Sx.F.H.* **10**(1), 1992, 23-8; **10**(2), 1992, 57-64; **10**(3), 1992, 89-94. Includes pedigree, 17-18th c.

Kniveton
See Chaworth

Kuffeler
DABNER, RALPH J. 'The Kuffelers in England', *R. & B.* **7**(1), 1980, 19-21. 17-18th c.

Kyme
CHALLEN, W.H. 'Kyme family of Lewes', *Sx.A.C.* **100**, 1962, 111-36. 15-17th c. Includes will of John Kyme, 1574.

La Warr
GODFREY, WALTER H. 'The La Warr family and Halnaker House', *Sx.A.C.* **82**, 1942, 59-64. Medieval.

Lade
WRIGHT, SIMON. 'Links between Kent and Sussex families in the 17th, 18th & 19th centuries', *Hindsight: the journal of the Uckfield & District Preservation Society* **2**, 1996, 64. See also **3**, 1997, 19. Lade, Nutt, & Fuller families, *etc;* includes folded pedigrees shewing connections.

Lambert
FARRANT, JOHN H. 'James Lambert, senior and junior, landscape painters of Lewes, *Sx.A.C.* **135**, 1997, 249-63. 18th c.
LAMBERT, UVEDALE. 'The Lambert of Blechingley', *E.Sy.F.H.S.J.* **5**(2), 1982, 25-31; **5**(3), 1982, 31. Includes pedigree, 16-20th c.
LAMBERT, UVEDALE. 'The Lamberts of Blechingley', *L.H.R.* **19**, 1980, 33-8. Includes pedigree, 16-20th c.
ROUND, J. HORACE. 'The tale of a great forgery', *Ancestor* **3**, 1902, 14-35. Lambert family of Surrey and Yorkshire, medieval.
Some account of the family of Lambert of Woodmansterne, Bansted, and other places in the County of Surrey. Privately printed, 1886. Brief; 14-19th c.
See also Baldy

Lanaway
HEWINS, MAURICE. 'John Lanaway and Lawrence Alderslade, yeomen', *F.M.S.Q.N.* **8**(6), 1988, 119-21. Includes pedigree of Lanaway, 17th c.

Lane
See Doble

Langridge
'Langridge', *D.P.H.S.M.* **2**(7), 1984, 20-24. 16-19th c.

Launder
See Msaster

Lavington
WILBERFORCE, ALAN. *Lavington: the history of a Sussex family.* Privately published, 1919. Medieval-19th c.

Lawrence
MANTHORPE, HEATHER. 'They were fishmongers in the Lambeth Walk', *E.Sy.F.H.S.J.* **18**(3), 1995, 9-11. Lawrence and Tyler families, 19th c.

Le Couteur
PHILLIPS, DON. 'Miss Le Couteur of Jersey', *F.M.S.Q.N.* **9**(2), 1990, 35-6. Includes pedigree shewing connection of Le Couteur and Sumner, 19th c.

Leaf
TAYLOR, DAVID C. 'The Leafs of Painshill', *E.L.H.S.N.* **58**, 1985, 7-9. See also **61**, 1986, 22-3.

Leaver
LEVER, R.A. 'A Surrey man looks at his ancestors', *Surrey history* **1**(4), 1976, 170-74. Leaver family of Richmond, *etc.,* 17th c.

Lee
See Brown(e)

Leedes
LLOYD, ELEANOR. 'Leedes of Wappingthorne', *Sx.A.C.* **54**, 1911, 37-54. Includes folded pedigree, 15-17th c.

Leete
BRIDGER, CHARLES. *The family of Leete, with special reference to the genealogy of Joseph Leete, esq., F.S.S., chevalier de la Legion d'Honneur, South Norwood, Surrey,* ed. J. Corbet Anderson. Privately published, 1881. Includes folded pedigree of 'Leete of South Norwood, County Surrey: a genealogy of the Eversden branch of Leete, of Cambridgeshire', 16-19th c.

Leigh

D., G.H. 'Leigh of Stockwell', *M.G.H.* **1**, 1868, 246. Undated pedigree.

LEVESON-GOWER, GRANVILLE. 'Notices of the family of Leigh of Addington, *Sy.A.C.* **7**, 1880, 77-123. Includes folded pedigrees, 14-18th c., extracts from parish registers, deed abstracts, wills, *etc.*

SWEETMAN, H.S.A. *A genealogical memoir of the ancient, honourable and extinct family of Leigh of Addington.* Privately printed, 1887. 14-18th c.

Lennox

KENT, JOHN. *Records and reminiscences of Goodwood and the Dukes of Richmond.* Sampson Low, Marston & Co., 1896. Lennox family, 17-19th c.

Leppard

LEPPARD, R.W. 'The Leppards: a Danehill and Horsted Keynes family', *D.P.H.S.M.* **3**(5), 1987, 32-7. 16-19th c.

'Hale House and the Leppard family', *D.P.H.S.M.* **6**(3), 1999, 25-7. At Danehill.

Leslie

BURN, MAURICE. 'Colenel Charles Leslie, 1788-1870', *Sx.F.H.* **8**(3), 1988, 121-6. Includes pedigrees, 19-20th c.

Lever

LEVER, R.A. 'The Lever family's 170 years in a Sussex village', *Sx.F.H.* **4**(1), 1979, 11-13. Of South Harting, 1729-1898.

LEVER, R.A. 'Proving an Elizabethan descent', *Family tree magazine* **10**(7), 1994, 11. Lever family.

Levett

COUPER, GILLIAN. 'Notes on the Levetts of Wilmington', *Sx.G.L.H.* **7**(2), 1985, 63. 18-19th c.

Lewer

TURNER, ROSEMARY. 'Full circle, or, researching in Lambeth', *E.Sy.F.H.S.J.* **21**(1), 1998, 21-3 & 42. Lewer family, 19th c.

Lewknor

COOPER, WILLIAM DURRANT. 'Pedigree of the Lewknor family', *Sx.A.C.* **3**, 1850, 89-102. 13-17th c.

HALL, EDITH M. 'Katherine Lewknor', *Sx.N.Q.* **13**, 1950-53, 256-7. Pedigree, medieval.

WAINEWRIGHT, JOHN B. 'Lewknor family', *Notes and queries* 12th series **5**, 1919, 201-2. Of Horsted Keynes, 16-17th c.

Lickfold

LICKFOLD, GORDON. 'Lickfold: a one-name study', *R. & B.* **6**(4), 1980, 137-40.

Lin(d)field

Longshot: journal of the Lin(d)field One Name Group. 1992- . Many articles on the Lin(d)field family.

LINDFIELD, ALAN G. 'The early Linfields', *Longshot: journal of the Lin(d)field One Name Group* **4**(1), 1995, 26-32. Medieval.

LINFIELD, MALCOLM. 'The Lin(d)field One Name Group', *Sx.F.H.* **11**(3), 1994, 103-4.

LINFIELD, ERIC. 'The Storrington Linfields and their poor relations of Sullington and Washington', *Longshot: journal of the Lin(d)field One Name Group* **2**(2), 1993, 56-61; **3**(2), 1994, 51-3, 19-20th c.

LINFIELD, MALCOLM. 'The West Sussex protestation returns 1641/2', *Long shot: journal of the Lin(d)field One Name Group* **3**(1), 1994, 18-27. Biographical notes on Linfield mentioned in them.

See also Penn

Linge

LINGE, ROBERT. 'Be wary of the census!', *F.R.* **5**(3), 1990, 56-7. Notes on the Linge family, 19th c.

Linton

See Morgan

Lintott

LOWER, MARK ANTONY. 'Family of Lintott', *Sx.A.C.* **8**, 1856, 275-6. 18-19th c.

Lloyd

'The geonealgeye of Henrey Lloyd ali's Rossindall of Cheyme in the com. of Surrey, esq.', *M.G.H.* **2**, 1876, 277-9. Of Rossendale, Lancashire, Derbyshire, and Cheam, Surrey, medieval-16th c.

See also Ragge

Lock

SERMONETA, DUCHESS OF. *The Locks of Norbury: the story of a remarkable family in the XVIIIth and XIXth centuries.* John Murray, 1940.

Locke King

PARDOE, B.F.J. 'The Locke King's', *Walton & Weybridge Local History Society paper* 3, 1969, 12-16. Locke King family, 18-20th c.

PULFORD, J.S.L. *The Locke Kings of Brooklands, Weybridge.* Walton & Weybridge Local History Society paper 31. 1996. 19-20th c., includes pedigrees of the families of King, Fortescue, Hoare, and Gore-Brown.

Long

HOWARD, ROBERT MOWBRAY, ed. *Records and letters of the family of the Longs of Longville, Jamaica, and Hampton Lodge, Surrey.* 2 vols. Simpkin Marshall Hamilton, Kent, & Co., 1925. Includes pedigrees, 17-20th c.

Longhurst

LONGHURST, DICK. 'Have I got the right one? *R. & B.* 23(4), 1997, 144-5. Longhurst family, 18th c.

Lowdell

BURCHALL, MICHAEL J. 'The Lowdell family', *Sx.G.L.H.* 1(4), 1980, 138-45. 17-20th c.

Lower

'The family of Lower', *Sx.A.C.* 22, 1870, 228-9. Brief note, medieval-19th c.

Lucas

POLS, ROBERT. 'The elusive James Lucas', *R. & B.* 11(2), 1984, 52-3. 18th c.

POLS, ROBERT. 'Poor Lucas', *R. & B.* 11(3), 1984, 94-5. See also 11(4), 1985, 135. Late 18th c. Lucas family.

Luck

'A Luck family bible ... ', *Sx.F.H.* 5(7), 1983, 222. Late 19th c. entries.

Lulham

See Acton

Lumley

HORTON-SMITH, L.G.H. 'A Sussex Lumley in search of a father three centuries ago', *Sx.N.Q.* 11, 1946-7, 8-13. See also 12, 1948-9, 28-33. 18th c.

Lun(d)sford

N., J.G. 'Pedigree of the family of Lunsford, of Lunsford and Wilegh, Co.Sussex', *Collectanea topographica et genealogica* 4, 1837, 139-56.

SHOOSMITH, EDWARD. 'Lundsfords of Whyly', *Sussex county magazine* 3, 1929, 238-42. 17th c.

Luxford

BAILEY, SUSAN. 'How I discovered my Sussex ancestry', *Sx.F.H.* 8(2), 1988, 59-60. Luxford family, 19th c.

Macdonald

MUNCEY, FRANCES. 'A remarkable family', *E.L.H.* 113, 1999, 6-10. Macdonald family, 19-20th c.

Machell

CHALLEN, W.H. 'John Machell, M.P. Horsham', *Sx.N.Q.,* 16, 1963-7, 114-21. Includes much information on his family, 16-17th c.

Maddockes

HOLDEN, E. LOFFT. 'Entries relating to the Maddockes family', *Genealogist* 3, 1879, 141-3. Of Suffolk and Surrey, 17-18th c.; includes will of Kinsman Singleman, 1769.

Madg(e)wick

BROWN, DAVID. 'The name of Madgwick', *Sx.F.H.* 13(7), 1999, 257. Discussion of variations of the name.

MADGWICK, HERBERT. 'Elizabeth Madgewick: a Sussex stray?' *Sx.F.H.* 13(1), 1998, 16. Of Compton, 17th c.

Malins

CLARKE, G. 'The Malins inheritance', *R. & B.* 15(2), 1988, 44-6. Includes pedigree, 19-20th c.

Mallett

See Grace

Malthus

WHITE, ADRIAN. 'The Malthus family of Albury', *R. & B.* **21**(3), 1994, 102-5.

Mandy

MUNCEY, FRANCES. 'The Mandy family, butchers of Eastbourne', *E.L.H.* **103**, 1997, 9-12; **104**, 1997, 11-13. 18-19th c.

Mangles

GALE, BOB. 'The Mangles family', *Send & Ripley History Society newsletter* **74**, 1987, 8 & 9. Includes pedigree, 18-19th c.

Marchant

KAY, JOHN. 'A Marchant/Hastings/Ellis/ Chapman family bible', *Sx.F.H.* **6**(7), 1985, 251-2. 19th c.

LEWIS, MARIE. 'The Marchant family', *E.L.H.S.N.* **71**, 1989, 7-13. 18-20th c., includes pedigree.

Marshall

MARSHALL, GEORGE W. 'The founder of Christ Church, Southwark', *Reliquary* **20**, 1879-80, 169-71. John Marshall; includes genealogical notes on the Marshall family of Surrey, 16-17th c.

Marten

MARTEN, A.E. 'The family of Marten of Sussex', *Sx.A.C.* **67**, 1926, 203-16; **68**, 1927, 245-62. 17-20th c.

MARTEN, A.E. 'The Marten family', *Sx.N.Q.* **13**, 1950-53, 295-6. 17th c.

MARTEN, RODNEY ELLIOTT. 'One law for the rich?' *Sx.F.H.* **7**(4), 1987, 152-3. Marten family of Winchelsea; includes pedigree, 18-19th c.

Martin

ROLSTONE, ANN. 'The Martins of Northiam', *H. & R.F.H.S.J.* **4**(1), 1989, 9-10. 20th c.

Master

MASTER, GEORGE STREYNSHAM. *Some notices of the family of Master, of East Langdon and Yotes in Kent, New Hall and Croston in Lancashire, and Barrow Green in Surrey, with appendices of abstracts of parish registers, monumental inscriptions, original documents and wills, together with notices of the families of Streynsham, Wightman, Launder, Hoskins, and Whalley, now repre- sented by that of Master.* Mitchell & Hughes, 1874. Includes folded pedigree, 18-19th c.

May

SMITH, RICHARD J. 'The May family of Richmond and the Lisbon factory', *R.H.* **16**, 1995, 36-46. Includes pedigree, 17-19th c.

Maycote

PULLEIN, CATHARINE. 'Maycote family', *Sx.N.Q.* **4**, 1933, 250-51. 15th c.

Mayo

MAYO, CHARLES HERBERT. *A memoir of the Rev. Richard Mayo, sometime minister of Kingston-upon-Thames together with an account of some of his descendants.* Sherborne: J.C. & A.T.Sawtell, 1912. 17-18th c.

Meachen

MEACHEN, G. 'The Meachen family of Petworth', *Petworth Society bulletin* **22**, 1980, 12-13. 18-19th c.

Medhurst

MEDHURST, L.A.J. 'Extracts from Laughton churchwardens account book', *F.R.* **6**(5), 1992, 9. Relating to the Medhurst family, mid-18th c.

Mercer

COLLINS, WILLIAM J., SIR. 'Some memorials of the Mercer family', *Transactions of the Baptist Historical Society* **7**, 1920-21, 22-30. Of Kent and Sussex, 17-19th c.

Mervyn

DRAKE, WILLIAM RICHARD, SIR. *Fasciculus Mervinensis, being notes historical, genealogical and heraldic of the family of Mervyn.* Privately printed, 1873. Of Wiltshire, Sussex, Devon, *etc.* Includes pedigrees, 16-19th c.

'Tabular pedigree of Durford Abbey branch of the Mervyn family', *M.G.H.* N.S. **1**, 1874, 422-6. Includes *inquisitions post mortem*, wills, extracts from Rogate parish registers, funeral certificates, *etc.*, 16-17th c.

Michelborne

ATTREE, F.W.T. 'Notes on the family of Michelborne', *Sx.A.C.* **50**, 1907, 61-108. See also 183-4. Includes folded pedigrees, 16-18th c., wills, *etc.;* of Horsted Keynes and Stanmer, Newick, Clayton, and Winchester.

Michell
ATTREE, F.W.T. 'Cuckfield families: the Michells', *Sx.A.C.* **53**, 1910, 109-28. See also **65**, 1924, 257-8. Includes folded pedigree, 16-17th c.

Midmore
BIGGS, JUNE. 'Who needs parish registers?', *North West Kent Family History* **6**(4), 1992/3, 111-4, Midmore family; includes pedigree, 15-17th c.

Miller
LOWER, MARK ANTONY. 'Notices of the family of Miller, of Burghill and Winkinghurst', *Sx.A.C.* **9**, 1857, 33-40. 17-18th c.

Millis
MILLIS, MARVIN. 'A Millis family of Kingston-on-Thames', *E.Sy.F.H.S.J.* **20**(4), 1997, 39-41. 19th c.

Milton
CLARKE, MIDGE. 'One hundred years of a Sussex public house *Sx.F.H.* **5**(3), 1982, 87-90. Milton family; includes pedigree, 18-20th c.

Mimms
MIMMS, PETER. *Only for life: a labouring family from Civil War to Second World War.* Bournemouth: the author, 1995. Of the East Midlands, Southwark, Bermondsey, and Devon, 17-20th c.

Mitchell
EVERSHED, P.B. 'Twice a Mrs. Evershed: a Mitchell family history', *Sx.F.H.* **8**(5), 1989, 198-9. 19-20th c.

Mizen
MORRIS, GERALD A. *The Mizens of Mitcham.* Merton Library Service, 1989. Includes pedigree, 19-20th c.

Moase
C., P. 'An old Petworth farming family', *Petworth Society bulletin* **22**, 1980, 10-11. Moase family, 19-20th c.

Molineux
MOLINEUX, GISBORNE. *Memoir of the Molineux family.* J.S.Virtue and Co., 1882. Of Sefton and Haughton, Lancashire, Nottinghamshire, Staffordshire, Sussex, and Ireland, medieval-19th c.

Molinier
'Molinier family', *Wandsworth notes and queries* **11**, 1899, 211-12. 18th c., of Wandsworth.

Molyneux
Memoir of the Staffordshire and Sussex families of the Haughton or Teversal branch of the Molyneux family. [ ]: Privately published, 1879. Brief.

Montacute
BURCHALL, M.J. 'Medieval family history: the Montacutes and dating a Battle Abbey deed', *Sx.F.H.* **13**(5), 1999, 155-9.

Montague
SALZMAN, L.F. 'Some Sussex Domesday tenants 1. Alured Pincerna and his descendants', *Sx.A.C.* **57**, 1915, 162-79. Montague family, 11-13th c.

Montgomery
FRANKLYN, CHARLES A.H. *A genealogical history of the families of Montgomerie of Garboldisham, Hunter of Knapp, and Montgomerie of Fittleworth.* Ditchling: Ditchling Press, 1967. Garboldisham, Norfolk; Knapp, Perthshire.

MASON, J.F.A. 'Roger de Montgomery and his sons (1067-1102)' *Transactions of the Royal Historical Society* 5th series **13**, 1963, 1-28.

Moore
PASSINGHAM, S. 'Any more for any Moore', *Petworth Society magazine* **59**, 1990, 12-13. Moore family of Petworth, 19th c.

TURNER, FREDERIC. 'Notes from an old diary: the Moores of Milton Place, Egham', *Notes & queries* 12th series **5**, 1919, 284-6; **6**, 1920, 15-16 & 118. 15-17th c; includes brief pedigree.

'Moore pedigree', *M.G.H.* **1**, 1868, 310-13. Of Essex and Surrey; 17-19th c.

See also Du Moulin-Browne

Morden
See Shurlock

More
MIDGLEY, WINIFRED. 'The More family and Farnham Castle', *F.M.S.Q.N.* **2**(12), 1971, 8-10. See also 3(2), 1972, 16. 16-17th c.

See also Bentley and Polsted

Morgan

LINTON, DAVE. 'But I don't want to be a Morgan!' *E.Sy.F.H.S.J.* **10**(1), 1987, 22-3. Morgan and Linton of Wandsworth, 18th c.

Morpeth

MORPETH, R.P. 'The Morpeths of Ruthwell', *R. & B.* **1**(1), 1974, 23-5. 18th c.

Morris

BURCHALL, MICHAEL J. 'A martyr-descent', *Sx.F.H.* **3**(5), 1978, 137-40. Morris family of Heathfield, Buxted, *etc.,* 15-20th c.

GILBERT, DEREK. 'The Morris family at Fernhurst, London Road', *Hindsight: the journal of the Uckfield & District Preservation Society* **1**, 1995, 28-9.

Morton

S[TEINMAN], G.S. 'Pedigree of Morton of Whitehorse, in the parish of Croydon, Surrey', *Collectanea topographica et genealogica* **3**, 1836, 169-71.

Mowcomber

'The Mowcombers: a French family in Sussex', *Sx.G.L.H.* **1**(1), 1979, 18-20. 16-17th c.

Mychell

'Stammerham', *Sx.N.Q.* **1**, 1926/7, 58-9. Brief note on the Mychell family, 16-18th c.

Myer

MYER, EWART. *Myers first century, 1876-1976: the story of Myers comfortable beds.* Horatio Myer & Co., 1976. Of Vauxhall; includes pedigree of Myer family, and many names of bed-makers.

Naldrett

EVERSHED, SAMUEL. 'The Naldretts of Naldrett, Rudgwick', *Sx.A.C.* **24**, 1872, 288-91. Includes folded pedigree, 16-18th c.

NALDRETT, R., & NALDRETT, K.E. *The family tree of the Naldretts of West Sussex.* Melksham: privately published, 1985. 16-20th c. pedigrees.

Napper

HADDOCK, C.A. 'The old Sussex family of Napper', *Sussex county magazine* **16**, 1942, 297. 16-19th c.

HADDOCK, C.A. 'More about old Sussex', *Sussex county magazine* **18**, 1944, 216. Napper family of Rudgwick and Ifold.

Needler

BAX, ALFRED RIDLEY. 'Henry Needler, a forgotten poet and philosopher of Surrey', *Sy.A.C.* **25**, 1912, 101-115. See also **26**, 1913, 140. Includes notes on his family, 17-18th c.

Nelson

EXCELL, PHYL, & EXCELL, STANLEY. 'Lord Nelson's relatives in Sussex', *Sx.F.H.* **4**(5), 1980, 165-9; **4**(6), 1980, 192-4. Includes pedigree, 18-19th c.

EXCELL, PHYLLIS, & EXCELL, STANLEY. 'Lord Nelson's relatives in Sussex', *Sx.F.H.* **14**(1), 2000, 28-33. Includes pedigree, 18-19th c.

Nesbitt

STEVENSON, JANET. 'Arnold Nesbitt and the origin of the Stevenson family of Winchelsea', *Sx.F.H.* **8**(7), 1989, 297-303. 18-19th c.

STEVENSON, JANET H. 'The Nesbitts of Norwood House: a footnote to Junius', *Sy.A.C.* **82**, 1994, 169-79. 18-19th c.

Nettlefold

CROFTON, C. ANTHONY. *The Nettlefolds: a genealogical account of the family of Nettlefold, settled in the County of Surrey by record from the 14th century, and in particular of the family and descendants of Edward Netylfold of Dorking, who was there buried 28th October 1581.* Lewes: Farncombe & Co., 1963

Nevill(e)

LAKIN, MARGARET. 'The Nevilles at Sheffield Place', *D.P.H.S.M.* **1**(9), 1981, 7-10. 17-18th c.

LAKIN, MARGARET. 'The Nevill(e)s at Sheffield Place', *D.P.H.S.M.* **5**(6), 1996, 22-6. 17-18th c.

NEVILL, EDMUND R. 'Neville of Combe Nevill (Surrey and Essex)', *Genealogist* N.S. **32**, 1916, 160-63. 13-16th c.

Newdegate

NICHOLS, JOHN GOUGH. 'The origin and early history of the family of Newdegate, so long as they remained connected with Surrey', *Sy.A.C.* **6**, 1874, 227-67. Includes appendix, 'Charters and abstracts of charters relating to Newdegate and the Newdegates'; also parish register extracts.

Newington

BAYNE, KIM. 'The history of a branch of the Newington family of Sussex', *Sx.F.H.* 7(1), 1986, 20-26. 16-19th c.

Newland

See Cobden

Newnham

NEWNHAM, C.J. *History of the Cross-in-Hand windmill and of the Newnham and Ashdown families.* Lewes: East Sussex Planning Department, 1979.

NEWNHAM, TOM. 'Tracing the surname Newnham', *Family tree magazine* 14(5), 1998, 9-10. Of Hampshire, Sussex, Kent, London, *etc.,* includes distribution maps.

'Newnhams', *D.P.H.S.M.* 2(7), 1984, 24-7. 17-19th c.

See also Way

Newton

GODFREY, WALTER H. 'Southover Grange and the Newton family', *Sx.N.Q.* **13**, 1950-53, 1-4. 16th c.

NOYES, T. HERBERT, C. 'Some notices of the family of Newton, of East Mascalls in Lindfield, and Southover Priory, near Lewes, and of Newton and Pownall Hall, in Cheshire', *Sx.A.C.* **9**, 1857, 312-42. Includes pedigrees, 14-19th c., also pedigree of Noyes of East Mascalls, 16-19th c.

Nixon

MUKERJI, JENNY. 'On account of a hammer', *R. & B.* 12(1), 1985, 8-10. Nixon family of Farnham, early 19th c.

Norfolk, Dukes of

See Howard

Norrell

HENRY, MICK. 'The surname Norrell in Sussex and Essex', *Sx.F.H.* **8**(8), 1989, 377-9. Includes pedigree, 19-20th c.

Norton

See Carrill and Drew

Noyes

See Newton

Nutt

COMBES, PAM. 'Oldlands furnace, Marshalls, and the Nutt family', *Wealden iron: bulletin of the Wealden Iron Research Group* 2nd series **16**, 1996, 13-16. 17th c.; includes descent of Oldlands 16-17th c.

See also Lade

Nye

CHALLEN, W.H. 'Nye family of Sussex and elsewhere', *Notes and queries* **206**, 1961, 284-8. 16-17th c.

WRIGHT, MICHAEL. 'Bodysnatcher to banker (or, side tracked in Kingston)', *R. & B.* 3(4), 1977, 115-7. Nye family, 19th c.

Oliver

OLIVER, JOHN. *My family in West Surrey.* [Haslemere]: Haslemere Educational Museum, 1995, Oliver family, 16-20th c.

Onslow

VULLIAMY, C.E. *The Onslow family, 1528-1874, with some account of their times.* Chapman & Hall, 1953. Of Clandon.

Osborn

OSBORNE, B.E. 'The Osborns, farmers from Telscombe, & the Bakers, brickmakers from Piddinghoe', *Sx.F.H.* 4(7) 1981, 209-11. 19th c.

See also Stedman

Owton

BEATTIE, ALAN. 'The Owtons of Bishopstone', *Sx.G.L.H.* 2(2), 1980, 63. 16-17th c.

Oxenbridge

BIRD, RUTH. 'Richard Oxenbridge of Horsted Keynes and his family, 1644-1719', *Sx.A.C.* **114** 1976, 325-6. Brief note.

COOPER, WILLIAM DURRANT. 'The Oxenbridges of Brede Place, Sussex, and Boston, Massachusetts', *Sx.A.C.* **12**, 1860, 203-20. 16-17th c., includes will of John Oxenbridge, of Boston, 1673-4.

Pagden

GINMAN, SUE. 'James William Pagden of Alfriston', *Sx.F.H.* **11**(8), 1995, 287-8. 19th c.

GINMAN, SUE. 'The Pagden family: tailors of Burwash', *Sx.F.H.* **12**(7), 1997, 249-50; **12**(8), 1997, 292. 19th c.

GINMAN, SUE. 'The Pagdens of Frog Firle', *Sx.F.H.* **12**(6), 1997, 211-12. 19th c.

Page

COUPER, GILLIAN M. 'The Page family of Wilmington', *Sx.F.H.* **10**(6), 1993, 222-4. 16-19th c.

COUPER, GILLIAN M. 'Stones that tell a story, 1', *F.R.* **8**(2), 1993, 44-5. Page family of Wilmington, 18th c.

THOMAS, J.R. 'The Page family of Wilmington: the saga continues', *Sx.F.H.* **11**(1), 1994, 17-18. 18-19th c.

Pain(e)

MONTAGUE, ERIC R. 'James Pain and Sons of Mitcham, manufacturers of fireworks (1872-1965)', *Surrey history* **4**(1), 1989/90, 35-48. Includes notes on the Pain family, 19-20th c.

PAINE, J. 'Help wanted', *Sx.F.H.* **10**(4), 1992, 137-8. Pedigrees of Paine, 19-20th c.

Palmer

[JENYNS, ROGER]. *The pedigree of the ancient family of the Palmers of Sussex, 1672, copied from the original ms. in the possession of Charles James Palmer esquire, of Dorney Court, together with extracts from registers, inscriptions on coffin-plates, etc., illustrating the Palmer genealogy.* Privately printed, 1867.

SCOTT, J.HOLFORD. 'The family of Palmer of Wokingham, and Rye', *Berks., Bucks., & Oxon archaeological journal* **23**, 1917, 29-31 & 62-4. Medieval-19th c.

'The pedigree of the antient family of the Palmers of Sussex, 1872', *M.G.H.* **1**, 1868, 105-22. 14-17th c.; shews connections with many other families.

Pankhurst

WILSON, PATRICIA. 'Four point five grandchildren', *H. & R.F.H.S.J.* **9**(3), 1994, 58-9. See also **9**(4), 1994, 70. Pankhurst family, 18-19th c.

Paris

BURGESS, DON. 'Being 90% sure', *Sx.F.H.* **9**(7), 1991, 253-5. Paris family; includes pedigree, 18th c.

Parker

BERRY, HARRY. 'The Parkers of Ratton', *Sx.G.L.H.* **3**(3), 1981, 101-6; **3**(4), 1981, 130-32. 14-18th c.

'The Parker descent', *E.L.H.S.N.* **83**, 1992, 14-16. 14-17th c.

See also Gage

Parris

BURGESS, DON. 'An interesting heirloom', *Sx.F.H.* **11**(1), 1994, 23-4. See also **11**(4), 1994, 141-2. Parris family, 19th c.

Parsons

THOMPSON, OLIVE ISABEL. 'My great-grandfather's quiverfull', *Sx.F.H.* **7**(6), 1987, 234-8. Parsons family; includes pedigree, early 19th c.

Passele

SAALER, MARY. 'The de Passele family and the manor of Alderstead', *L.H.R.* 1983, 11-16. Medieval; includes pedigree.

SALZMAN, L.F. 'The widows of Sir Edmund de Passele', *Sx.N.Q.* **6**, 1936-7, 140-42. Early 14th c.

Passifull

See Boxall

Patching

HOAD, RONALD J. 'The Patchings of Shipley', *Sx.F.H.* **9**(6), 1991, 203-4. 19th c.

HOAD, R.J. 'The Patchings of Shipley: another episode', *Sx.F.H.* **10**(1), 1992, 3-5. 19-20th c.

Pattenden

TAYLER, KAREN. 'Pattenden/Prevett connections', *Sx.F.H.* **12**(7), 1997, 250. Includes pedigree, 18-20th c.

Payne

MARKWICK, JOHN. 'Eastbourne's old town post office: a family's century of service', *F.R.* **9-10**, 1995-6, *passim*. Payne family, 19-20th c.
See also Bax

Pears

CHESTER, JOSEPH LEMUEL. 'Pears or Peirce of Richmond, Co.Surrey', *M.G.H.* N.S. **3**, 1880, 71-2. 17th c.

Pechell

BURRELL, PERCY, SIR. 'Castle Goring', *Sx.A.C.* **26**, 1875, 113-51. Pechell family; includes pedigree, 16-19th c.

Peckham

PACKHAM, MAURICE. 'Arms and the man', *Sx.F.H.* **12**(7), 1997, 243-5. Peckham family, medieval.

PECKHAM, W. D. 'Dallaway's pedigrees', *Sx.N.Q.* **6**, 1936-7, 190-91. Corrects Dallaway's pedigree of the Peckham family, 17-18th c.

Peirce

See Pears

Pelham

E., W.S. 'Pelham: a doubtful pedigree', *Genealogist* **4**, 1880, 213-25. See also **5**, 1881, 105-6. Of Sussex; 13-14th c.

LOWER, MARK ANTONY. *Historical and genealogical notices of the Pelham family.* Privately printed, 1873. Medieval-19th c.

LOWER, MARK ANTONY. 'The Norman origin of the family of Pelham', *Sx.A.C.* **24**, 1872, 183-8. Includes pedigree, 11-13th c.

MCLEAN, DAVID. 'Sussex and the U.S.A. second series no.7: Sussex and the Pelhams of Boston, Massachusetts', *Sussex County magazine* **5**, 1931, 674-9. 18th c.

PELHAM, ARTHUR, MRS. & MCLEAN, DAVID. *Some early Pelhams.* Hove: Combridges, 1931. 13-17th c., includes folded pedigree.

Pellatt

PHILLIPS, MABERLY. 'Pedigree and genealogical memoranda relating to the family of Pellatt, of Steyning, Bignor, Bolney, Ardingly, Lewes and Staplefield, Co.Sussex, Bletchingly and Croydon, Co.Surrey, and Staines, Co.Middlesex', *Sx.A.C.* **38**, 1892, 99-128; **39**, 1894, 55-93. Includes folded pedigrees, 13-19th c., will abstracts, extracts from parish registers, etc.

Pelling

RAYNER, JULIA. 'Pelling otherwise Young', *Sx.F.H.* **8**(4), 1988, 169-73. Includes pedigree, 18-20th c.

Pendrell

MARSHALL, A.E. 'The Sussex Pendrells', *Sx.F.H.* **6**(4), 1984, 127-35. 17-19th c.

Penn

LINFIELD, WILLIAM. 'William Penn and the Quaker Linfields of Sussex', *Longshots: journal of the Lin(d)field One Name Group* **3**(2), 1994, 42-51. Includes pedigree, 17-18th c.

Percy

BATHO, GORDON. 'The Percies at Petworth 1574-1632', *Sx.A.C.* **95**, 1957, 1-27.

Perior

WOODS, P. 'The family of John Perior, charter-warden of Godalming, and the manor of Ashurst in Godalming', *Sy.A.C.* **21**, 1908, 113-24. See also **22**, 1909, 196; **24**, 1911, 173-6. Includes folded pedigree, 15-17th c.

Perring

PERRING, RALPH, SIR,& KNIGHT, MICHAEL. 'Perrings in Surrey and Knights of Reigate: an illustrated history of two family firms', *Surrey history* **3**(5), 1988/9, 203-15. Includes notes on the families of Knight, 18-20th c., and Perrings, 19-20th c.

Peverell

SHOOSMITH, EDWARD. 'The Peverells: a crusading family', *Sussex county magazine* **3**, 1929, 457-62. See also 586-7, 665, 741-2 & 808. Medieval.

Philcox

MAY, GWEN. 'Discovering the Philcoxes of Hartfield', *Sx.F.H.* **8**(1), 1988, 37-8. 19-20th c.
See also Baldy

Phillips

BROOMAN, RONALD C. 'Notes on the Phillips family of East Sussex', *H. & R.F.H.S.J.* **4**(3), 1989, 51-7. 18-20th c.

HANNON, D. *The Phillips family of Brighton.* Harrison & Sons, 1938. Not seen.

Pilbeam

PILBEAM, NORMA. 'James Pilbeam of Chiddingly, mercer, *Sx.F.H.* **9**(4), 1990, 127-31. Pilbeam family, 17-18th c.

PILBEAM, NORMA. 'The Pilbeams of Chichester', *Sx.F.H.* **7**(4), 1987, 136-44. Includes pedigree, 16-17th c.

Pilfold

'Pedigree of Pilfold, Sussex', *M.G.H.* N.S. **4**, 1884, 85. 16-19th c.

Pim

PIM, F.W. 'The Pim family in Canada & ancestors from Sussex', *Sx.F.H.* **6**(4), 1984, 140-43. 16-19th c.

Pincerna

See Montague

Pinckney

SLATFORD, JOHN. 'An 18th century American family in Ripley', *Send & Ripley History Society newsletter* **108**, 1993, 2-3; **111**, 1993, 6-7. Pinckney family.

Pissaro

REID, MARTIN. 'The Pissaro family in the Norwood area of London: where did they live?' in LLOYD, CHRISTOPHER, ed. *Studies on Camille Pissaro.* Routledge & Kegan Paul, 1986.

Pix

HOVENDEN, ROBERT, & HARDY, ALFRED LLOYD. 'Pedigree of the family of Pix of Hawkhurst, Kent, and Ewhurst and Northiam, Sussex', *M.G.H.* 2nd series **5**, 1894, 111-6. 16-19th c.

'Genealogical notes relating to the family of Pix', *M.G.H.* 2nd series **5**, 1894, 17-19, 43-6, 56-9 & 110. Of Kent and Sussex; includes 17th c. pedigree, wills, and monumental inscriptions.

Plaistead

PLAISTEAD, ARTHUR H. *The Plaistead family of North Wilts., with some account of the branches of Berks., Bucks., Somerset, and Sussex.* Westminster Pub. Co., 1939.

Plank

PLANK, DENNIS. 'Is he George or John?' *R. & B.* **24**(4), 1998, 149-50. Plank family, 19th c.

Plumstead

'Copy of a register relating to the Plumstead family, late of Brixton, Co.Surrey, written on the fly-leaf of an old bible in the possession of Edward Waltham, esq., of Stockwell Green', *M.G.H.* N.S., **1**, 1874, 131. 18-19th c.

Pollard

WIGAN, MARY. 'A soldier's life', *Sx.G.L.H.* **5**(3), 1983, 109-10. Settlement certificate of John Pollard, 1826; includes pedigree.

Polsted

EVANS, JOHN. 'An account of the presents received and expenses incurred at the wedding of Richard Polsted of Albury, esquire, and Elizabeth, eldest daughter of William More of Loseley, esquire", *Archaeologia* **36**(1), 1855, 33-52. Albury is in Hertfordshire. Includes many names.

Poole

BRENT, JUDITH. 'The Pooles of Chailey and Lewes: the establishment and influence of a gentry family', *Sx.A.C.* **114**, 1976, 69-80.

Poppy

KESINGLAND, ADAM CHARLES. 'A Poppy by any other name: a remarkable tale uncovered', *Family tree magazine* **12**(10), 1996, 4-5. Poppy als Kesingland, early 20th c.

Porter

CARTER, JENNIFER. 'The Surrey side of the family', *R. & B.* **18**(4), 1992, 140-41. Porter family; includes pedigree, 18-20th c.

Portman

RUTTON, W.L. 'The Portman family at Kew', *Notes and queries* 10th series **5**, 1906, 383-4. Primarily a Somerset family.

Poulter
POULTER, S.R.C. 'Some notes on the Poulters',
P.L.D.L.H.S. 4(4), 1980, 97-102. Includes
pedigree, 16-17th c.

Poyles
See Puilles

Poynings
COOPER, WILLIAM DURRANT. 'Settlement
previous to the marriage of Isabella
Poynings with William de Cricketot, 1343',
Sx.A.C. 14, 1862, 182-5. 14th c., with notes
on the Cricketot family.
ROUND, J.H. 'The Lords Poynings and St.
John', *Sx.A.C.* 62, 1921, 1-20. Medieval.

Poyntz
MACLEAN, JOHN, SIR. *Historical and
genealogical memoirs of the family of
Poyntz, or, eight centuries of an English
house.* Exeter: William Pollard, 1886.
Includes pedigrees, medieval-19th c., of
Curry Malet, Somerset, North Ockendon,
Essex, Iron Acton, Gloucestershire,
Reigate, Surrey, Benefield,
Northamptonshire, *etc.*

Prevett
See Pattenden

Priaulx
WOODROOFFE, SELINA MARY. 'Pedigree of
Priaulx', *M.G.H.* 3rd series 2, 1898,
81-7 & 125-32. Of Hampshire, Sussex,
Surrey, *etc.;* pedigree, monumental
inscriptions, wills, Chancery papers, *etc.,*
17-18th c.

Prichard
See Bax

Prinseps
MCALL, TOM. 'More about the Prinseps of
Pevensey Bay, 1897-1937', *E.L.H.S.N.* 68,
1988, 9-15. 19-20th c.

Prior
See Fogden

Pruce
See Spruce

Puilles
BONNER, ARTHUR. 'The de la Puilles and the
Poyles', *Sy.A.C.* 41, 1933, 124-6. 13-14th c.

Purcel
BROOKS, E. ST.JOHN. 'Catteshill and another
usher serjeanty in the Purcel family',
*Bulletin of the Institute of Historical
Research* 10, 1932-3, 161-8. 12th c.

Pursglove
GOOCH, A.L. 'The Pursgloves of the
Congregational Chapel at Herstmonceux',
Sx.F.H. 7(2), 1986, 46-8. 17-18th c.

Pyecroft
RICHARDSON, MICK. 'The Pyecrofts of
Petworth', *Petworth Society magazine* 77,
1994, 34-7. Late 19th c.

Ragge
'The Ragge, Lloyd and Walker families,
Leatherhead saddlers and harness makers
from the 17th to the 20th century',
P.L.D.L.H.S. 2(5), 1961, 144-54. Includes
pedigree.

Ravenscroft
See Hall

Read
HOWCUTT, FRANCIS. 'Read: an elusive family
in London', *North West Kent family
history* 5(3), 1989, 90-91. Of Walworth
and Bermondsey, 19th c.

Rees
See David

Reynolds
See Fogden

Rice
DOUGLAS. 'Rice family', *M.G.H.* 3rd series 1,
1896, 101. 18th c.

Richardson
RICHARDSON, HENRY. 'Henry the Bad and
Henry the Good', *H. & R.F.H.S.J.* 5(1),
1990, 3-7; 5(2), 1990. 32-4. Richardson
family of Hailsham and Australia,
19-20th c.

Richmond
See Engleheart

Richmond, Dukes of
See Lennox

Ridge
GORING, JEREMY. 'A Sussex dissenting family: the Ridges of Westgate Chapel, Lewes', *Sx.A.C.* **129**, 1991, 195-215. 17-19th c., includes pedigree.

RIDGE, DUDLEY. *A Sussex family: the family of Ridge from 1500 to the present day.* Phillimore & Co., 1975. Includes pedigrees, wills, *etc.*

RIDGE, J.C., & BURCHALL, M.J. *The Ridge family of Sussex.* Occasional papers **2**. [Brighton]: Sussex Genealogical Centre, 1979. Reprinted from *Sx.G.L.H.* **1**(3), 1979.

RIDGE, JESSIE C. 'Ridge family of Sussex', *Sx.F.H.* **10**(3), 1992, 111-17; **10**(4), 1992, 155-62; **10**(5), 1992, 201-6. 17-20th c.

RIDGE, J.C., & BURCHALL, M.J. 'Ridge family of Sussex', *Sx.G.L.H.* **1**(3), 1979, 89-98. 16-20th c.

SAWYER, JOHN. 'Notes on the Ridge family, being some extracts from *a book of memorandums* kept by William Ridge, 1715-1785', *Sx.A.C.* **37**, 1890, 116-32. See also **38**, 1892, 228.

Roberts
COMBER, JOHN. 'Marriage chains', *Sx.N.Q.* **3**, 1931, 60-62. Marriages of Joan Roberts with May, Alfrey, Giles and Busbridge, 17th c.

POWELL, EDGAR. 'Roberts and Horde families', *Genealogist* N.S. **2**, 1885, 46-7. Roberts of Willesden, Middlesex; Horde of Ewell, Surrey, includes pedigree, 16th c.

TYLER, J.W. 'Roberts of Borzell in Ticehurst, Sussex', *M.G.H.* 5th series **7**, 1929-31, 99-109. Includes pedigree, 15-19th c.

Robinson
ROBINSON, A.W. 'A famous firm of Sussex shipowners: the story of the Robinsons of Littlehampton', *Sussex county magazine* **12**, 1938, 30-32 & 91-5. 19th c.

Rochester
RENSHAW, WALTER C. 'The Rochesters of Selmeston and Jevington, Co.Sussex', *Genealogist* N.S., **22**, 1906, 209-11. 17-18th c.

Rogers
BASTIAN, F. 'Leatherhead families of the 16th and 17th centuries, IV. Rogers of the Rectory', *P.L.D.L.H.S.* **2**(4), 1960, 103-12. Includes folded pedigree.

'Rogers', *M.G.H.* 4th series **2**, 1908, 50. Pedigree, 17th c.

Rose
MARYON, ALLAN J. 'The IGI and Richard Rose', *R. & B.* **20**(4), 1994, 157-8. Of Chobham, 18th c.

Roser
See Weston

Rossetti
IDEN, RON. 'The Rossettis at Aldwick', *B.R.L.H.S.* **32**, 1995, 27-30. 19th c.

TITMAN, LILY. 'The Rossettis in Sussex', *Sussex county magazine* **15**, 1941, 384-6. 19-20th c.

Rossindall
See Lloyd

Rothes, Earl of
See Evelyn

Rowe
ROBINSON, CHARLES J. 'Rowe family', *M.G.H.* **1**, 1868, 166-8. Of Sussex and London; pedigree, 16-18th c., with wills.

TURNER, EDWARD. 'A brief sketch of the history of John Rowe, esqre, and his descendants, with a copy of his will', *Sx.A.C.* **24**, 1872, 85-98. Includes pedigree, 16-19th c.

'Rowe pedigree', *M.G.H.* **1**, 1868, 162. 16-17th c.

Rowed
BATCHELOR, JUDITH A. 'The Roweds of the North Downs', *Family history* **18**(149); N.S., **125**, 1996, 175-82. Of Kent and Surrey; includes pedigree, 18-19th c.

Rowland

BURCHALL, MICHAEL J. 'The Rowlands of Horsham', *Sx.G.L.H.* 1(2), 1979, 65-71.

Rudge

See Turner

Russell

CHESTER, J.A. 'The Russell family of Lewes & Wyndham Hospital', *Sussex history* 2(6), 1983, 32-4. 17-18th c.

LOOSEMORE, JOSÉ. *Where they have trod: a story of Sussex shoemakers.* Lewes: CGB Books, 1998. Russell family; includes pedigree, 18-20th c.

RUSSELL, PAMELA. 'Mr. Russell of White Street and his relatives', *Baptist quarterly* N.S., **28**, 1979-80, 373-83. Southwark family, 18th c.

Sackville

DICK, G.R.A. 'The Sackvilles of Withyham', *Sussex county magazine* **13**, 1939, 113-8. 17th c.

HASSALL, W.O. 'The Sussex property of St. Mary, Clerkenwell, and the Sackvilles', *Sx.N.Q.* **11**, 1946-7, 38-40. 14-16th c.

HESS, ROBERT L. 'The Sackville family and Sussex politics: the campaign for the by-election, 1741', *Sx.A.C.* **99**, 1961, 20-37.

MONCREIFFE, IAIN, SIR. 'The Sackvilles of Buckhurst', *Armorial* **2**, 1960-61, 33-41 & 131-8. Medieval-20th c.

See also Etchingham

St. John

BRANSGROVE, STEPHEN. 'The St. John family of Battersea', *Wandsworth historian* **43**, 1984, 10-14. Includes pedigree, 15-18th c.

EVANS, CHARLES F.H. 'The family of St. John of Lambeth, *Sy.A.C.* **63**, 1966, 151-6. See also **65**, 1968, 144-7. 16-17th c., includes will abstracts.

See also Poynings

Saleman

'A medieval ancestor: the early Salemans', *Sx.G.L.H.* 2(1), 1980, 27-30.

Salmon

SALMON, JOAN, & SALMON, PAT. 'A fisherman named Salmon', *H. & R.F.H.S.* 11(1), 1996, 6-7. Of Hastings, 19th c.

Sands

BASTIAN, F. 'Leatherhead families of the 16th and 17th centuries, III. Sands of Randalls', *P.L.D.L.H.S.* 2(3), 1959, 76-84. Includes pedigree.

DALTON, ANNE. 'Hawksden Forge, Mayfield and the Sands family', *Wealden iron: bulletin of the Wealden Iron Research Group* 2nd series **18**, 1998, 39-47. Includes pedigree, 17th c.

Sanxay

SANXAY, THEODORE F. *The Sanxay family, and descendants of Rev. Jacques Sanxay, Huguenot refugee to England in sixteen hundred and eighty-five.* New York: privately printed, 1967. Of Devon, Surrey, Sussex, *etc.*

Sargent

TICKNER, VINCENT. 'You can go back two hundred years quite simple, can't you?' *Sx.F.H.* **10**(7), 1993, 273-80. Sargent family; includes pedigree, 18-20th c.

Sassoon

DANE, MICHAEL. *The Sassoons of Ashley Park.* Walton on Thames: the author, 1999. Includes pedigree, 18-20th c.

JACKSON, STANLEY. *The Sassoons.* William Heinemann, 1968. Of Ashley Park, 19-20th c.; includes pedigrees.

WALKER, MICHAEL L. 'The manor of Batailles and the family of Saunder in Ewell during the 16th and 17th centuries: the owners of the manor of Batailles to the end of its tenure by the Saunder family', *Sy.A.C.* **54**, 1955, 76-101. Includes pedigree shewing relationship of Saunder and Carew, 15-17th c.

'Extract from the pedigree of the family of Saunders of Ewell in the county of Surrey', *M.G.H.* 5th series **8**, 1932-4, 109-18. 15-17th c.

Sawyer

THOMPSON, DON. 'The Sawyers of Uckfield', *Hindsight: the journal of the Uckfield & District Preservation Society* 5, 1999, 28-35. Includes pedigree, 18-20th c.

Scawen

See Blunt

58

Scrase

LOWER, MARK ANTONY. 'Genealogical memoir of the family of Scrase', *Sx.A.C.* **8**, 1856, 1-16. Includes pedigrees, 16-19th c.

RENSHAW, WALTER C. 'Notes on the Scrase family of Co.Sussex', *Genealogist* N.S., **20**, 1904, 217-21. 15-18th c.

SCRASE, R.L. 'The origins of the name of Scrase', *Sx.F.H.* **5**(5), 1983, 141-2. Medieval.

SCRASE, LESLIE. *Some Sussex and Surrey Scrases.* West Molesey: the author, 1987. Medieval-20th c.

Scutt

HODSOLL, VERA. 'Looking for the Reverend Thomas Scutt', *E.L.H.* **85**, 1992, 8-12. See also **86**, 1992, 10-12. Scutt family, 19th c.

Selden

BOOKER, K. 'Searching for Seldens', *F.R.* **4**(2), 1989, 34-6.

ELLIS, W.S. 'Lineage of John Selden', *Sx.A.C.* **8**, 1856, 271-2. 16-17th c.

Sellon

EVANS, C.F.H. 'The Sellon family', *R. & B.* **2**(3), 1976, 103-6. 17-18th c.

Selwyn

BAZELEY, WILLIAM. 'Some records of Motson in the County of Gloucester, and of the Selwyns', *Bristol and Gloucestershire Archaeological Society transactions* **2**, 1877/8, 241-84. Includes pedigrees of Selwyn of Sussex and Gloucestershire, 15-19th c.

CODRINGTON, R.H. 'Notes on the traditional connexion of the Sussex and the Gloucestershire families of Selwyn', *Sx.A.C.* **38**, 1892, 163-5. 14-16th c.

Sergison

LOWER, MARK ANTONY. 'Some notices of Charles Sergison, esq., one of the Commissioners of the Royal Navy, *temp* William III and Queen Anne, and his family connections', *Sx.A.C.* **25**, 1873, 62-84. See also 226 & 234-5; **26**, 1875, 272-3. Includes folded pedigree of Sergison (and Warden), 16-19th c.

Sex

HAYWARD, NINA. 'The more Sex the better!' *R. & B.* **13**(1), 1986, 8-10. Sex family; includes pedigree, 19th c.

PERRIS, COLIN. 'The Sex family', *Send & Ripley History Society newsletter* **128**, 1996, 8-10. See also **130**, 1996, 8-10. Includes pedigree, 18-20th c.

Shaw

See Willoughby

Shayer

STEWART, BRIAN, & CUTTEN, MERVYN. *The Shayer family of painters.* F. Lewis, 1981. Of Chichester and Southampton, *etc.;* includes pedigree, 18-20th c.

Shelley

DJABRI, SUSAN CABELL, et al. *The Shelleys of Field Place.* Horsham: Horsham Museum Society, 2000. 17-19th c.; includes pedigrees.

EXCELL, PHYL, & EXCELL, STANLEY. 'A poet and his family: Percy Bysshe Shelley', *Sx.F.H.* **5**(3), 1982, 94-100. See also **5**(4), 1982, 131. Includes pedigree, 18th c.

FORMAN, H. BUXTON. 'Pedigree of Percy Bysshe Shelley', *M.G.H.* N.S. **3**, 1880, 421-6. 17-19th c.

STEVENS, F. BENTHAM. 'The exodus from Sussex of the Shelleys', *Sx.N.Q.* **17**, 1968-71, 1-9. See also 62. 17-20th c.

Shepherd

See Collins

Sherlock

'Sherlock', *D.P.H.S.M.* **2**(7), 1984, 27-8. 19th c.

Sherson

COX, A.D. 'The Sherson family of Fetcham', *P.L.D.L.H.S.* **3**(7), 1973, 190-204. Includes pedigree, 17-19th c.

Shier

SMITH, GEORGE H. 'The Shiers of Slyfield and the contents of the Slyfield chest', *P.L.D.L.H.S.* **1**(4), 1950, 9-14. Medieval-18th c.

Shurley

TURNER, EDWARD. 'Isfield Place, with notes respecting the family of Shurley', *Sx.A.C.* **18**, 1866, 124-36. 16-17th c.

Shurlock

'Surrey wife of a Sussex gentleman: Shurlock/Morden', *Sx.F.H.* **6**(2), 1984, 55-6. 18-19th c.

Sicklemore

MARNEY, JOAN T. DE. 'My Sussex ancestors, mainly Sicklemores', *Sx.F.H.* **7**(3), 1986, 90-93. Includes pedigree, 16-19th c.

Siddall

EDWARDS, MARION. 'This modestly educated girl from Southwark: the family background of Elizabeth Siddall', *Family history* **10**, 1979, 189-98.

Sidney

BEVINS, ALAN. 'Was the Sidney's first home in Surrey?' *R. & B.* **6**(2), 1979. 55-7. Medieval.

SIDNEY, PHILIP. *Memoirs of the Sidney family.* T.F.Unwin, 1899. Not seen.

SYDNEY, PHILIP. *The Sidneys of Penhurst.* S.H.Bousfield & Co., 1901. Revised edition of the *Memoirs.* Includes pedigree.

Simmons

LEWIS, MARIE. 'Charles Frederick Simmons of Simmon's and Cowley's dairies', *E.L.H.S.N.* **43**, 1982, 3-4. See also **44**, 1982, 2; **45**, 1982, 5-6. Simmons family, 19-20th c.

Singleman

See Maddockes

Skeete

BASTIAN, F. 'Leatherhead families of the 16th and 17th centuries, 1. The Skeete family', *P.L.D.L.H.S.* **2**(1), 1957, 6-14. Includes pedigree, 16-17th c.

Slaughter

'Leaves from a tree', *Sx.F.H.* **1**(1), 1973, 15. Brief pedigree of Slaughter family, 18-19th c., from entries in a family bible.

Slyfield

HARVEY, JOHN H., & SLYFIELD, GORDON N. *Slyfield Manor and family of Great Bookham, Surrey.* Horsham: Springfield Press, 1959. 13-17th c.

Smith

BEADEN, J.A. 'My Sussex ancestors', *Sx.F.H.* **12**(1), 1996, 31-4. Smith of Graffham, 19th c.

DAWE, DONOVAN. 'The Smiths of Selsdon Park', *L.H.R.* **19**, 1980, 23-8. 19th c.

The three Smiths, brothers and painters, natives of Chichester: exhibition at the Pallant House Gallery, 3rd May to 3rd August 1986. Chichester: Friends of Pallant House, 1986. Includes a biography of the Smith brothers by Sibylla Jane Flower.

See also Baldy and Griffiths

Smyth

'[Henry Smyth of Peper Harrow]', *Sy.A.C.* **32**, 1919, 161-2. Brief note on his ancestry, 16th c.

Snashall

BURCHALL, MICHAEL J. 'The Snashall family: Quakers and blacksmiths', *Sx.G.L.H.* **2**(1), 1980, 11-14. 17-18th c.

Snow

DAVIS, CECIL T. 'Snow family of Wandsworth', *M.G.H.* 3rd series **4**, 1902, 250-51. Pedigree, *etc.,* 16-17th c.

Soal

LOVE, LIZZIE. 'Will power: don't just say who say where!' *Sx.F.H.* **13**(7), 1999, 245-7. Soal family; includes pedigree, 18-20th c.

Spark(e)s

BODDINGTON, REGINALD STEWART. *Genealogical memoranda relating to the Sparks and Tickell families.* Privately printed, 1877. Pedigree of Sparks of Byfleet, Surrey; 18-19th c., also of Tickell of various counties.

BODDINGTON, REGINALD STEWART. 'Sparks pedigree', *M.G.H.* N.S. **2**, 1877, 469-72. 18-19th c.

See also Carrill

Spencer

MILWARD, RICHARD. *The Spencers in Wimbledon, 1744-1944.* Milward Press, 1996.

Spice

SPICE, MARY. *From Sussex to the south land: the saga of Saul and Sarah Spice and some of their descendents.* [York, W. Australia]: M. Spice, 1991. Includes pedigree, 17-20th c. The 'south land' of the title is Australia.

Spooner

BURN, MAURICE. 'The Spooner-Elliott-Burn connection', *Sx.F.H.* **8**(1), 1988, 24-6. Includes pedigree, 18-20th c.

Springate

SPRINGATE, BRENT. 'A One Name Study Group', *Sx.F.H.* **11**(4), 1994, 146-7. Springate family.

SPRINGATE, BRENT. 'Springate Alley, Lambeth', *E.Sy.F.H.S.J.* **19**(4), 1996, 42-3. Springate family, 19-20th c.

Springett

LOWER, MARK ANTONY. 'Sir William Springett & the Springett family', *Sx.A.C.* **20**, 1868, 34-46. Includes pedigree, 17-18th c.

SALMON, E.F. 'Plumpton and the Springett family', *Sx.A.C.* **56**, 1914, 199-200. Includes brief pedigree, 17th c.

'Springett family', *Blackmansbury* **1**(2), 1964, 21-4. 17th c.; of Ringmer, *etc.*

Spruce

PRUCE, JOHN. 'A (S)Pruce one-name study', *E.Sy.F.H.S.J.* **21**(1), 1998, 18-20. 18-19th c.

Stanford

THOMAS-STANFORD, CHARLES. *The descent of the family of Stanford of Preston, Sussex.* Chiswick Press, 1907. Brief; includes folded pedigree, 16-19th c.

YEOMAN, W. JEREMY. 'The Stanford family and their residences in Godstone and Lingfield', *E.Sy.F.H.S.J.* **17**(3), 1994, 8-12. 16th c.

Stapley

HARWOOD, H. W. FORSYTH. 'The Baronetcy of Stapley', *Genealogist* N.S. **18**, 1902, 140-62. 17-18th c.; includes wills, monumental inscriptions, extracts from parish registers, *etc.*

TURNER, EDWD. 'On the domestic habits and mode of life of a Sussex gent in the 17th and early part of the 18th century', *Sx.A.C.* **23**, 1871, 36-72. Stapley family of Hickstead Place, Twineham.

S., J.C. 'The Stapleys of Hickstead', *Sx.A.C.* **48**, 1905, 158-9. Extracts from bishops transcripts for Twineham, 1606-99.

Stedman

ALLESTON, JAMES. 'Petworth clockmakers: Stedman of Petworth', *Petworth Society bulletin* **20**, 1980, 12-13. 19th c. Also includes list of Petworth clockmakers, 18-20th c.

JONES, JOHN. 'Stedman alias Osborn, 1750-1850', *Sx.G.L.H.* **3**(4), 1981, 125-6.

Stevens

VOLLOR, ANN M. 'The Stevens of Willingdon', *Sx.F.H.* **7**(6) 1987, 249-50. Includes pedigree, 19th c.

Stevenson

See Nesbitt

Stilwell

STILWELL, MARTIN. *A history of the Stilwells of Surrey.* Privately published, 1999. Medieval-20th c.

Stint

TYLER, J.C. 'Stint or Stynt', *M.G.H.* 5th seres, **6**, 1926-8, 209-12. Of London and Surrey; pedigree, 16-18th c., with wills.

Stockman

See Griffiths

Stopham

ROUND, J.H. 'The Stophams, the Zouches, and the Honour of Petworth', *Sx.A.C.* **55**, 1912, 19-34. Medieval.

Stoughton

O., H.N. 'Family of Stoughton', *New England historical & genealogical register* **5**, 1851, 350. Pedigree, 16-17th c.

Strawson
BOND, STELLA. 'Does anyone want a family?' *Family tree magazine* **12**(7), 1996, 21-2. Strawson family of Newbury and Streatham.

Streater
JENKYN, F.M. 'The Streater family', *Sx.F.H.* **8**(8), 1989, 375-6. 18-20th c.

Streynsham
See Master

Stroud
BECKETT, GWEN. 'The Stroud family of Farnham', *F.M.S.Q.N.* **6**(9), 1983, 194-5. 20th c.

Strudwick
KENYON, G.M. 'A Sussex yeoman family as glassmakers', *Sx.N.Q.* **7**, 1938-9, 171-3. See also 248-9. Strudwick family, 16-18th c.

Strugnell
STRUGNELL, RICHARD. 'The family of Strugnell, manorial tenants', *E.Sy.F.H.S.J.* **17**(1), 1994, 17-21. 18-19th c.

Sturt
TYLER, J.C. 'Sturt', *M.G.H.* 5th series **6**, 1926-8, 193-4. Of Ripley; pedigree, 17-18th c.

Stynt
See Stint

Sumner
See Le Couteur

Tamplin
TAMPLIN, RICHARD. 'The Phoenix Brewery', *Sx.F.H.* **11**(1), 1994, 20. Brief note on the Tamplin family of Brighton, 19-20th c.

Tanner
NEVE, CHARLES. 'Tanner', *M.G.H.* N.S. **3**, 1880, 52. See also 55-6. Of Sussex; pedigree, 17-19th c.

Tasker
TASKER, BRIAN. 'The Tasker family and Summersales Farm', *Sx.F.H.* **8**(4), 1988, 164-5. At Withyham; 17-19th c.

Tauke
POST, J.B. 'The Tauke family in the fourteenth and fifteenth centuries', *Sx.A.C.* **111**, 1973, 93-107. Of Sussex and Hampshire.

Taylor
A[LLESTON], J. 'Taylor family of clockmakers, Petworth', *Petworth Society bulletin* **21**, 1980, 18-19.

BARKER, R.H. 'Which grandfather?', *E.Sy.F.H.S.J.* **1**(3), 1978, 21-2. Taylor family, 19th c.

Teague
GOWER, GRAHAM CROSSINGHAM. 'Teggeherugge and Teghe: a surname origin', *Sx.F.H.* **12**(4), 1996, 146-8. Origins of Teague surname.

Tellick
See Griffiths

Tester
See Gibb

Thatcher
SPOKES, P.S. 'Thatcher family', *Sx.N.Q.* **4**, 1933, 126. See also 159 & 189. 16-17th c.

Thomas
HODSOLL, VERA. 'Some notes on Ratton, Willingdon and Eastbourne-Parker manors, part 2: the Thomases to 1847', *E.L.H.* **84**, 1992, 18-22, 18-19th c. Continued by 'part 3. The Thomases after 1847', *E.L.H.* **85**, 1992, 6-8.

Thomason
GLOVER, DOROTHY J. 'The Thomasons of Westham', *Sx.N.Q.* **16**, 1963-7, 331-3. 16-17th c.

Thompson
TEBBUTT, C.F. 'The church of Sir Richard de Wych and the Thompson family of Ashdown Park, Hartfield', *Sx.A.C.* **118**, 1980, 389-92. Includes pedigree, 19-20th c.

Thornton
HIGGINS, D.A. 'The Thorntons of Dorking: clay tobacco pipe makers', in DAVEY, PETER, ed. *The archaeology of the clay tobacco pipe, IX: more pipes from the Midlands and Southern England.* B.A.R. British series **146(i)**. B.A.R., 1985, 423-33. Includes pedigree, 18-19th c.

Thrale

HYDE, MARY. *The Thrales of Streatham Park.* Cambridge, Massachusetts: Harvard University Press, 1977. 18-19th c.

WILLIAMS, M.Y. 'The Thrales of Streatham', *Lambethan quarterly* **15**, 1966, 4-5. Brief note, 18-19th c.

Threele

CHALLEN, W.H. 'Threele family', *Sx.N.Q.* **15**, 1958-62, 91-5. 16-17th c.

Thunder

BEDINGFIELD, G.M. 'Never beleve anything without checking twice! (Thunder family)', *Sx.F.H.* **6**(2), 1984, 60-62. 19th c.

Tickner

TICKNER, VINCENT. 'Proving the origins of a Tickner ancestor from Westfield', *R. & B.* **24**(1), 1997, 15-17. 18-19th c.

TICKNER, VINCENT. 'Lost in the Johns', *R. & B.* **14**(3), 1987, 92-5. Tickner family, 16-17th c.

TICKNER, VINCENT. *An introduction to the Tickner family in North-West Surrey up to the twentieth century.* Family history series **1**. Brighton: G.A.M.C.O. Publications, 1986. 16-20th c.

TICKNER, VINCENT. *The Tickners: their distribution before 1600 and their origins.* Family history series **2**. Brighton: G.A.M.C.O. Publications, 1987. Of Surrey, Sussex, Kent, etc.

TICKNER, VINCENT. 'The Tickners of Send and Horsell (1570-1765)', *Send & Ripley History Society newsletter* **79**, 1988, 11-12; **81**, 1988, 9-10; **83**, 1988, 5-6; **84**, 1989, 6-8. 16-18th c.

Tidey

RAFFERTY, MERLE. 'A death bed legacy and two death bed confessions', *Sx.F.H.* **13**(4), 1998, 138-9. Tidey family, 19th c.

RAFFERTY, MERLE. 'The Tideys of Worthing and Washington', *Sx.F.H.* **11**(1), 1994, 10-11. 18th c.

TIDEY, MERLE. *The Tideys of Washington, Sussex, 1773-1973.* Bala: Dragon Books, 1973. Includes pedigrees, 18-20th c.

Tilbury-Tarner

WARDEN, STEPHEN. 'The Tilbury gig': the story of the Tilbury-Tarner family of Brighton', *Sx.F.H.* **4**(6), 1980, 186-9. 19-20th c.

Tickell

See Sparks

Tollemache

ROUNDELL, CHARLES, Mrs. *Ham House: its history and art treasures.* 2 vols. George Bell & Sons, 1904. Family history of the Tollemache family, Earls of Dysart, 17-19th c.

Tomsett

'Tomsett', *D.P.H.S.M.* **2**(7), 1984, 28-32. 19th c.

Torr

MCQUIRE, SYLVIA. 'Father, dear father', *R. & B.* **11**(2), 1984, 49-51. Torr family, 19-20th c.

Towner

TOWNER, REG. 'A concise history of the Towner family', *Sx.F.H.* **13**(8), 1999, 266-7. 17-18th c.

TOWNER, R. 'Towner: a Sussex surname', *Sx.F.H.* **8**(4), 1988, 174-6. Origins of the surname.

Tradescant

ALLAN, MEA. *The Tradescants: their plants, gardens and museums, 1570-1662.* Michael Joseph, 1964. Of Henstead, Suffolk, Meopham, Kent, and Lambeth, *etc.*

LEITH-ROSS, PRUDENCE. *The John Tradescants, gardeners to the rose and lily queen.* Peter Owen, 1984. Includes pedigree, 16-17th c.

Travers

SIDES, HENRY J. 'The Travers family, of Chaldon, Surrey', *Sy.A.C.* **3**, 1865, 353. Brief note, 16th c.

Trayton

G., W.H. 'Trayton of Lewes sketch pedigree', *Sx.N.Q.* **3**, 1931, 250-52. 16-18th c.

Trecothick
TICKNER, VINCENT. 'The Trecothick family and Addington Place, (1768-1802)', *E.Sy.F.HS.J.* 16(4), 1993, 11-14.

Tredcroft
DJABRI, SUSAN. 'The Tredcrofts of Horsham: confusion among the records', *Sx.F.H.* 13(7), 1999, 250-54. Includes pedigree, 15-17th c.

Tregoz
SALZMAN, L.F. 'Tregoz', *Sx.A.C.* 93, 1955, 34-58. Includes pedigrees, 12-14th c.

Tribe
ALLESTON, JAMES. 'Petworth clockmakers: notes on John Tribe', *Petworth Society bulletin* 19, 1980, 12-13. Tribe family, 18-19th c.

Tritton
TRITTON, J. HERBERT. *Tritton: the place and the family.* Arthur L. Humphreys, 1907. Of Kent, Surrey, *etc.;* medieval-19th c.

Tully
See Bax

Turner
ARNOLD, F.H., & CROIX, W. DE ST. 'Memoir of the Rev. E. Turner, M.A., V.P.', *Sx.A.C.* 25, 1873, 213-9. Includes folded pedigree, 17-19th c.
PENNINGTON, JANET. 'Turner family of Steyning', *Sx.F.H.* 6(6), 1985, 203-11. 17th c.
WOOD, P.D. 'The old firm', *Bulletin of the East Grinstead Society* 44, 1988, 4-6. History of Turner, Rudge & Turner, surveyors, with notes on the families, 18-20th c.
SALZMAN, L.F. 'Philip Turner', *Sx.N.Q.* 16, 1963-7, 37-40. Notes from a family bible, 18-19th c.
'Turner', *D.P.H.S.M.* 2(7), 1984, 32-4. 17-19th c.
See also Chaloner

Twine
GODFREY, WALTER H. 'Thomas and Brian Twine', *Sx.N.Q.* 2, 1929, 197-201 & 229-33; 3, 1931, 40-42 & 82-4. See also 250. Of Lewes, 16-17th c.

Tyler
See Lawrence

Uvedale
LEVESON-GOWER, GRANVILLE. 'Notices of the family of Uvedale of Titsey, Surrey, and Wickham, Hants.', *Sy.A.C.* 3, 1865, 63-192. Reprinted as LEVESON-GOWER, GRANVILLE. *Notices of the family of Uvedale of Titsey, Surrey, and Wickham, Hants.* Cox & Wyman, 1865. Includes pedigree, 14-17th c., wills, and rental of Crowhurst, Titsey and Tatlesfelde, 1401.

Vallence
MIDDLETON, JUDY. 'The Vallences of Brighton and Hove', *Sx.G.L.H.* 6(3), 1984, 98-103; 6(4), 1985, 141-50. 18-19th c.

Vaughan
BELLEWES, G.O. 'Vaughan family, Southwark', *M.G.H.* 5th series 2, 1916-17, 160. Extracts from family bible, 18th c.
N., N. 'A Southwark family', *Genealogical magazine* 7, 1903-4, 164-5. Vaughan family, 18-19th c.

Venis/Veness
BEATTIE, ALAN M. 'Isaac Veness', *Sx.F.H.* 12(5), 1997, 168-75. Includes pedigrees of Venis/Veness, 17-20th c.

Ventham
INKEL, D.W. 'Ventham, coachbuilder of Leatherhead and Dorking', *P.L.D.L.H.S.* 5(7), 1994, 179-83. Ventham family, 19-20th c.

Vernon
GROSSET. LENI. '[Pedigree of Vernon]', *F.M.S.Q.N.* 6(10), 1983, 215-6. 17-18th c.

Verrall
LUCAS, PERCEVAL. 'The Verrall family of Lewes', *Sx.A.C.* 58, 1916, 91-131. 18-19th c.
VERRALL, MICHAEL S. 'The Verrall surname', *Sx.F.H.* 8(1), 1988, 27-8. Medieval-17th c.

Vincett
VINCETT, ROBERT. 'A cut above the rest: ten generations of family butchers in East Sussex & Kent', *Sx.F.H.* 5(4), 1982, 127. Vincett family, 16-20th c.

VINCETT, R. '240 years of a Sussex family', *Sx.F.H.* **6**(3), 1984, 92-5. Vincett family, 18-20th c.

Vine

BIGGS, JUNE. 'A long line of carpenters', *North West Kent family history* **4**(2), 1986, 47-50. Vine family of Laughton, 17-18th c.

Wagner

WAGNER, ANTHONY, & DALE, ANTONY. *The Wagners of Brighton.* Phillimore, 1983. Includes folded pedigree, 17-20th c.

WAGNER, ANTHONY R. 'The Wagners of Brighton and their connections', *Sx.A.C.* **97**, 1959, 35-57. Includes folded pedigree, 17-20th c. Corrected in:

WAGNER, ANTHONY R. 'The Wagners of Brighton and their connections', *Sx.N.Q.* **15**, 1958-62, 173.

Wakeford

WAKEFORD, JOHN. 'John Wakeford of Deane', *R. & B.* **6**(2), 1979, 55-6. 18th c.

Waleys

MARTIN, DAVID, et al. 'Three moated sites in North-East Sussex, part 2. Hawksden and Bodiam', *Sx.A.C.* **128**, 1990, 89-116. Includes note on 'Hawksden and the Waleys family', by Nigel Saul. Medieval; the Bodiam section of the articles has no genealogical interest.

See also Etchingham

Walker

See Ragge

Walters

'Walters pedigree', *M.G.H.* N.S. **3**, 1880, 226-7. Of Somerset and Surrey, 17-19th c.

Waltham

See Plumstead

Walwyn

See Bullen

Warden

COOPER, J.H. 'Cuckfield families: the Wardens', *Sx.A.C.* **49**, 1906, 89-104. 17-18th c.

See also Sergison

Ware

BESWICK, MOLLY. 'Brickmaking at Ridgewood', *Hindsight: the journal of the Uckfield & District Preservation Society* **3**, 1997, 4-10. Ware family, 18-20th c.

Warenne

ANDERSON, FREDA. '*Uxor mea:* the first wife of the first William of Warenne', *Sx.A.C.* **130**, 1992, 107-29. 11th c.

BLAAUW, W.H. 'Warenniana: ancient letters and notices relating to the Earls de Warenne', *Sx.A.C.* **6**, 1853, 107-28. Medieval.

Washington

MCLEAND, DAVID. 'Sussex and the U.S.A. 1: Sussex and the Washingtons', *Sussex county magazine* **4**, 1930, 47-58. 17-18th c.

Waterer

LOWTHER, A.W.G. 'The Waterer family of Ashtead circa 1660 to 1790', *P.L.D.L.H.S.* **2**(2), 1958, 53-8. Includes pedigree, with 'A schedule of the records of the Waterer family of Ashtead'.

Waters

KING, JOHN. 'The Waters family', *E.Sy.F.H.S.J.* **4**(1), 1981, 19-20. Of Redhill, early 20th c.

Watson

WATSON, ROSEMARY. 'The Watsons of Woldingham', *L.H.R.* **28**, 1989, 12-20. 19-20th c.

Way

WAY, HERBERT, W.L. *History of the Way family: a record in chronological order of members of the Way family ...* Harrison & Sons, 1914. Includes pedigree of the Newnham family of Maresfield.

Webb

COUPER, G.M. 'Four generations, 1819-1970', *Sx.F.H.* **10**(1), 1992, 10-12. Webb family.

Week(e)s

FORD, JOHN M.T., ed. *A medical student at St. Thomas's Hospital, 1801-1802: the Weekes family letters.* Medical history supplement **7**. Wellcome Institute for the History of Medicine, 1987. Includes pedigree of the Weekes family of Hurstpierpoint, Sussex, 18-19th c.

JENNER, IRENE. 'William Weeks, coastguard, 1818-1903', *R. & B.* **13**(4), 1987, 142-6. Weeks family.
'Weeks chronological chart', *R. & B.* **14**(1), 1987, 19-21. Weeks family 1787-1941.
See also Wyke

Weller
WALKER, D. RAYMOND F. 'Thomas Weller, potter of Brede, his forebears and descendants', *Sx.F.H.* **12**(2), 1996, 67-71; **12**(3), 1996, 114-8; **12**(4), 1996, 155-8; **12**(5), 1997, 182-4; **12**(6), 1997, 236-9; **12**(7), 1997, 274-8; **12**(8), 1997, 295-8. Includes pedigrees, 18-19th c.

Wells
HAREFIELD, T.J. *Wells: a family history.* 2nd ed. The author, 1988. Of Shefford, Bedfordshire, London, Surrey, etc. Includes pedigree, 17-20th c.

Wenban/Wenbourne
WENBAN, A.A. 'Country to town: an illustrative account of the Wenban family', *Sx.F.H.* **4**(4), 1980, 136 & 144. 19th c.
WENBAN, A.A. 'A Wealden family', *Kent Family History Society journal* **1**(3), 1975, 55-7. Wenban family, 18-19th c., in Kent and Sussex.
WENBAN, A.A. 'Wenbans Farm, Wadhurst, Sussex, and the family name linked with it', *Sx.A.C.* **113**, 1975, 195-6. Wenban or Wenbourne family, 13-17th c.

Wepham
See Whapham

West
BRANSON, J.W. 'The West family of Farnham', *F.M.S.Q.N.* **2**(2), 1969, 10-12. 18-19th c.

Weston
HARRISON, FREDERIC. 'Sutton Place, Guildford', *Sy.A.C.* **9**, 1888, 1-18. Includes brief account of the Weston family, 15-18th c.
ROSER, BRIAN. 'When your name is not your name', *Sx.F.H.* **13**(6), 1999, 183-8. Weston and Roser families, 18-20th c.
WESTON, RODNEY VICTOR. 'The Weston family', *Hindsight: the journal of the Uckfield & District Preservation Society* **1**, 1995, 8-11. Includes pedigree, 18-20th c.

Whalley
See Master

Whapham
ELLIS, C.W. 'Discovering the Whaphams', *Sx.F.H.* **10**(1), 1992, 6-9; **10**(2), 1992, 49-53; **10**(3), 1992, 85-7; **10**(4), 1992, 129-30; **10**(5), 1993, 173-7. 17-20th c.
ELLIS, C.V. 'Nominally obscure: from Wepham to Whapham', *Sx.F.H.* **9**(6), 1991, 219-22. Whapham family, 16-19th c.

Wheeler
'Wheelers', *D.P.H.S.M.* **2**(7), 1984, 34-6. 18-19th c.

Whistler
WHISTLER, ROSE FULLER. 'The annals of an English family', *Sx.A.C.* **35**, 1887, 61-88. Whistler family, 13-19th c.

Whitaker
KING, H.W. 'A brief memoir of Admiral Sir Edward Whitaker, Knt.', *Sy.A.C.* **8**, 1883, 211-8. Includes 'pedigree of Whitaker, of Carshalton, Co.Surrey, and Soho Square, London', 18th c.

White
LEGGE, W. HENEAGE. 'Delves House, Ringmer, with some account of Gilbert White and his relatives there residing', *Reliquary and illustrated archaeologist* N.S. **6**, 1900, 1-14.
MANNING, ELFRIDA. 'Tanyard House and the Whites', *F.M.S.Q.N.* **7**(2), 1984, 26-8. At Farnham, includes pedigree, 15-16th c.
RICE, R. GARRAWAY. 'Genealogical memoranda relating to the family of White of Horsham, Steyning, Shipley, and Cowfold, Co.Sussex, of Mitcham, Croydon, and Reigate, Co.Surrey, and of London, with pedigree', *Sx.A.C.* **34**, 1886, 127-66. 16-19th c.; includes wills.
See also Whyte

Whitebread
PENNINGTON, JANET, & SLEIGHT, JOYCE. 'The Whitebread family of Jessops, Daylands, and Muggeridges: 17th and 18th century farmers of Ashurst and Wiston, West Sussex', *Sx.A.S.N.* **40**, 1983, 333-5; **42**, 1984, 377.

66

Whitef(i)eld
LOWER, MARK ANTONY. 'Notes on the family of Whitfeld, or Whitfield, of the Counties of Northumberland and Sussex', *Sx.A.C.* **19**, 1867, 83-90. Includes pedigree, 13-16th c.

Whitgift
THRELFALL, JOHN. 'Portrait of a lady: Jane (Whitgift) Bradbury', *Sy.A.C.* **78**, 1987, 176-7. Includes notes on Whitgift and Bradbury families, 16-17th c.

Whyte
CURTIS, HENRY J. *Pedigrees of Whyte or White, of Farnham, Co.Surrey; Aldershot, South Warnborough and Basingstoke, Co.Hants., and Hutton, Co.Essex, and a note on the Yateley cup.* The author, 1936. Reprinted from *Notes and queries* **171**, 1936, 110-16, 128-31, 146-51, 164-8 & 182-7. See also 395. 15-19th c.

Wightman
See Master

Wilde
See Bicknell

Wilkinson
SHAW, TONY. 'Roehampton House', *Wandsworth historian* **32**, 1982, 8. Brief note on the Wilkinson family, late 18th c.

Williams
N., N. 'Williams of Ewell', *Genealogical magazine* **7**, 1904, 108. Of Ewell Park, Epsom, 18-19th c.

Willoughby
HIGSON, P.J. 'The barony of Willoughby of Parham, *Genealogists magazine* **15**(1), 1965-8, 1-14. Descent to Leigh, Dawes, Fisher and Shaw *etc.*, 16-20th c.
PINK, W.D. 'The Barony of Willoughby of Parham', *Genealogist* **4**, 1880, 34-49.

Wilson
SHAW, HERBERT. 'Wilson the teaman', *E.Sy.F.H.S.J.* **5**(1), 1982, 21-3. Of South Croydon, 19th c.

BLENCOWE, ROBERT WILLIS. 'Paxhill and its neighbourhood, with extracts from the manuscripts of the Wilson family', *Sx.A.C.* **11**, 1869, 1-49. See also: 'Pedigree of Thomas Wilson, esq', *Sx.A.C.* **12**, 1870, 240-41. 15-19th c.

Winckton
See Baldy

Windever
'Windever notes', *M.G.H.* 2nd series **2**, 1888, 122-3. Of Surrey; extracts from family bible, 18th c.

Wing
THOMAS, J.R. 'Two brothers, such different lives: the story of John and Thomas Wing', *Sx.F.H.* **11**(1), 1994, 31-3. 19th c.
THOMAS, J.R. 'Who was Uncle Wing?' *Sx.F.H.* **9**(3), 1990, 90-92. Wing family; includes pedigree, 19th c.

Wisdom
UNDERWOOD, DAVID. 'The Wisdoms of Glynde', *Sx.F.H.* **8**(6), 1989, 258-60. Includes pedigrees. 18-20th c.

Wise
KEATS, SHEILA. 'A Victorian mystery (or skeletons in the family closet)', *Folkestone Family History Society journal* **1**(4), 1978-9, 32-5. Wise family of Lambeth, 19th c.

Wode
SMITH, J. CHALLENOR. 'John Wode, Speaker of the House of Commons, 1482-4', *Genealogist* N.S., **36**, 1920, 129-32. 13-14th c.

Wonham
THOMPSON, CHARLES. 'The Wonham family in Newdigate', *R. & B.* **14**(2), 1987, 50-53. Includes pedigree, 16-20th c.

Wood
BUTTON, P.R. 'Where are the silver teaspoons?' *H. & R.F.H.S.J.* **6**(4), 1992, 82-3. Wood family, 18-19th c.
See also Cranmer

Woodcock
See Bellingham

Woodroffe
'Pedigree of Woodroffe of Poyle Park,
Surrey', *M.G.H.* N.S. 1, 1874, 411-15. 16-
19th c.

Wright
NASH, S.G. 'Wrights of Brighton', 5(7), 1983,
229-31. 19th c.

Wyatt
JUPP, EDWARD BASIL. *Genealogical
memoranda relating to Richard Wyatt of
Hall Place, Shackleford, citizen and
carpenter of London, with an account of
the almshouse of his foundation at
Godalming, under the care of the
Company of Carpenters.* Cox & Wyman,
[1870?] Includes pedigree, 17-18th c.
JUPP, EDWARD BASIL. 'Richard Wyatt and his
almshouses', *Sy.A.C.* 3, 1865, 277-323.
Wyatt family of London, Middlesex and
Surrey; includes pedigree 17-19th c., many
Wyatt family wills, extracts from registers
of Puttenham and Isleworth, *etc.*
WYATT, H.P. 'Family of Wyatt', *Sx.A.C.* 13,
1861, 303-4.

Wyke
ELLIS, W.S. 'Wyke or Weekes of Kent and
Sussex', *Genealogist* 1, 1877, 192-3 & 222-
5. See also 2, 1878, 95-6.

Wyndham
WYNDHAM, H.A. *A family history, 1688-1837:
the Wyndhams of Somerset, Sussex and
Wiltshire.* Oxford University Press, 1950.

Young
EVERSHED, P.B. 'Who was John Young of
Goring? *Sx.F.H.* 13(2), 1998. 35. Young
and Evershed families, 17-18th c.
See also Pelling

Zillwood
SAMUEL, RUTH. 'Five unhappy women',
Sx.F.H. 11(8), 1995, 293-5. Zillwood and
Churcher families, 19-20th c.
SAMUEL, RUTH. 'Great-Grandma was a
Zillwood', *Sx.F.H.* 9(5), 1991, 166-9.
Includes pedigree, 18-19th c.

Zouche
See Stopham

Author Index

70

71

Family Name Index

Important

This is an index to sections 1-4 only. It does not include the numerous names listed in section 5. Since the latter are in alphabetical order, it would be superflous to include them here.

Place Name Index

77